What an INTELLIGENCE AGENCY will never tell you

60 key facts

CAROLINA RAMÍREZ
@MujerSeguridad

INDEX

Preface
Presentation
Introduction
Chapter 1: The World of Intelligence Agencies
- What are intelligence agencies for?
- Espionage, the second oldest profession in the world
- Value of intelligence: Data is the new oil
- *Books / movies and series – 60 key facts*

Chapter 2: The Pillars of Intelligence
- Information gathering
- Analysis of data
- Intelligence generation
- *Books / movies and series – 60 key facts*

Chapter 3: Intelligence Operations and Global Security
- Counterintelligence
- Counterterrorism
- Cyber intelligence
- *Books / movies and series – 60 key facts*

Chapter 4: Challenges, Controversies and Ethical Dilemmas
- Innovative Methods in Intelligence Management
- Big data and data analysis
- Metadata and Big Data: Similarities and Differences
- *Books / movies and series – 60 key facts*

Chapter 5: Intelligence, Transparency and Accountability
- Power is not unlimited and intelligence agencies know it
- Electronic communications monitoring: The good, the beautiful and the ugly

- Metadata and Big Data: The challenge of data access and management
- *Books / movies and series – 60 key facts*

Chapter 6: Intelligence is in Fashion
- Opportunities for people with talent in data analysis
- Boost your career with online training resources
- Unlock your future with scholarships and facilities

EXTRA BONUS: 60 KEY FACTS THEY WILL NEVER TELL YOU
- How to read and download complete books for free
- How to watch full movies and series for free
- Applications and other resources

Conclusion
Additional resources

PREFACE

With this daring and brave publication by the security professional Carolina Ramírez, or as she has rightly been named in our society, **La Mujer Seguridad**, she makes available to anyone who understands the real importance of intelligence services in organized societies, the tools to understand and analyze everything that involves the hidden parts of the successes or failures in the security policies of the nations that have democracy as a regime.

In her book, Dr. Ramírez Herrera addresses the different historical processes that have forced the adaptation of the tools of the intelligence agencies of States with political regimes, increasingly committed to the protection of human rights and accountability. Likewise, it highlights the importance of good and efficient security services, to keep the foundations that support nations firm, ready to face the new threats that loom over each of the nations that play their role on the world stage.

This work becomes a key piece, which currently fits together like a perfect chessboard the efforts of good intelligence analysis in accordance with the initiatives of each nation, in relation to its interests and the achievement of National Objectives.

Supported by her quality and professional experience, Carolina calls us to complement everything she expresses in her 274 pages (which I had to read on a Sunday afternoon) with a compilation of "Additional Resources" that contains:

26 Recommended books

> **25 Suggested** movies
> **25 Must-see** series
> **05 Training** portals
> **23 Scholarship** platforms
>
> **60 Platforms** and portals for movies, series, books, tools and *software's.*

We have in our hands a kind of log very useful for consulting, for analyzing and to provoke reflections that forge in the reader their own criteria about the importance of these tools, which, when used properly, would allow the objectives of the intelligence agencies to be achieved more effectively, in benefit of our nations and each citizen in particular.

Admiral (r) Sigfrido Pared Pérez, ARD

PRESENTATION

Get ready to delve into the intriguing world of intelligence agencies with "What an Intelligence Agency Will Never Tell You: 60 Key Facts"! This book is not only aimed at those familiar with the security field, but goes much further. It is designed to reach leaders, opinion makers and curious citizens who want to understand the critical role these agencies play in our dynamic and ever-evolving world.

The author, Carolina Ramírez, also known as @mujerseguridad, combines her experience of more than two decades in the field of security with a practical and accessible approach to demystify the complex universe of intelligence agencies. With the added value of those **60 key facts you should know**, the text offers a unique and revealing view of how these agencies directly influence our security, privacy, and the daily decision-making of every important global leader.

But this book goes beyond mere information. It is a tool that you can use as a guide, a resource to strengthen your skills and your understanding of the world around us. Each key piece of information is a door to deeper knowledge, an opportunity to reflect on the transcendent role that these agencies play in society and in our lives.

So, get ready for a journey of learning, curiosities and discovery that will challenge your perceptions and open your eyes to this world that remains hidden from the sight of many, full of practical and accessible resources, that you can legally take advantage of in your daily and professional life.

CAROLINA RAMÍREZ

Join this exciting exploration and discover what really happens behind the closed doors of intelligence agencies!

INTRODUCTION

I welcome you to **"What an intelligence agency will never tell you: 60 key facts"**. This book is a window into an intriguing and complex world that influences fundamental aspects of our daily lives. My name is Carolina Ramírez, known as @mujerseguridad, and it is a pleasure to be your guide on this discovery journey.

The idea is to imagine an informal conversation in some pleasant place, enjoying a good coffee, while I try to provide answers to some common doubts and concerns about intelligence agencies. My goal is **to simplify the complex**, demystify these thousand-headed monsters, without sacrificing the depth you deserve and offer you a tool that enables you to understand how their actions influence decision-making that impacts entire nations.

Over the past two decades, I have dedicated my career to understanding how these agencies shape countries' global security. Now, I want to share with you everything I have learned, **in clear and accessible language.**

It's not just about facts and figures, but about understanding how the actions of these agencies have a tangible impact on our daily lives. From keeping our communities safe to protecting our personal information, these organizations play a crucial role that often goes unnoticed.

Throughout these pages, I invite you to explore with me the lesser-known aspects of these mysterious organisms, maintaining a **practical and close approach**. This book is not just a passive read, but a tool that will empower you to better understand the world of intelligence and take advantage of the opportunities that a profitable and fulfilling career can offer you.

As an extra bonus, in a special chapter I will reveal to you the **60 key facts** that an intelligence agency will never tell you. This information will allow you to access a wide range of books, movies, series, management tools and other applications legally and for free. In addition, you will discover online digital television services, streaming of sporting events and other additional resources that will enrich your knowledge and entertainment without spending a single cent.

Let's begin this journey of learning and discovery!

CHAPTER 1: THE WORLD OF INTELLIGENCE AGENCIES

Intelligence agencies operate in a kind of parallel universe, a world where information is the most powerful weapon and shadows matter more than light. Amid this chaos, secrets that define the destiny of entire nations are protected.

In this chapter, I will reveal to you the very essence of these mysterious organisms, exploring their definition, function and evolution throughout history, their importance in today's global context and, as if this were not enough, you will be surprised at how they affect your daily life.

What are intelligence agencies for?

In a world where information is power, how do leaders know what to do in difficult situations? Intelligence agencies, those centers of strategic knowledge and guardians of national security play a vital role in the complex board of the geopolitical game. They provide **key information**, in a **timely manner**, that helps leaders **make informed decisions** for the security of the State and its citizens.

What really are intelligence agencies and what is their role in the world of national and international security? These organizations are the eyes and ears of a country, responsible for **collecting**, **analyzing** and **processing** critical information for strategic decision-making. From preventing terrorist threats to protecting national interests, their work is essential to the **security** and **stability** of a nation.

However, its role goes beyond mere data collection. They are a type of artisans who transform scattered information into useful and actionable intelligence reports for **political**, **military** and **police leaders**. They act as the first line of defense in the fight against organized crime, terrorism and other threats anywhere in the world.

In all the important decisions that are made daily in your country, they took into account some report from these organizations. From information gathering to intelligence analysis and production, these agents work tirelessly, maintaining a low profile to protect the national interest and ensure the safety and well-being of the population. They are like expert baristas who meticulously prepare **a perfect coffee**, combining the right ingredients for the best possible result, even though the customer who enjoys it may never see their faces.

Although maintaining these agencies involves a significant cost, the value they provide is incalculable. Ultimately, intelligence spending is an investment in the stability and security of society, and its absence could cost much more, both in economic terms and in human lives. Therefore, while the debate over funding them is valid, the question is not whether we can afford to keep them, but whether we can afford not to.

So, next time you read the news or hear about important political decisions, remember that behind it all are people working night and day to keep us safe. They are like that reliable companion who is always there when you need them, but their work is much bigger and has an impact on the entire society. Therefore, let us extend our recognition for the valuable work carried out by intelligence agencies in each country.

Espionage, the second oldest profession in the world

The history of intelligence agencies is fascinating and spans from ancient times to today's digital age. From manual strategies to innovative technologies, each stage has left an indelible mark on the way nations seek and use information to ensure their security and protect their interests.

From the ingenious tactics of **Sun Tzu** in ancient China to the arts of Roman military intelligence, the search for information for strategic decisions has been a constant recognized by masters of history. This interest in data has been the common thread that has defined intelligence networks over time.

In ancient biblical stories, intriguing episodes illustrate the use of espionage, intelligence, and secret missions in the pursuit of divine and earthly goals. Starting with **Joseph** accusing his brothers of being spies, **Moses** sending on missions and receiving intelligence reports from **Joshua and Caleb**, or the prostitute **Rahab** negotiating protection, in a joint operation, between the first and second oldest professions – **prostitution** and espionage.

A compelling example takes us to Ancient Greece, where the tyrant Histiaeus used **cryptography** in an innovative way by tattooing a message on the head of his slave to send a secret message to his compatriots in Miletus, in modern-day Turkey.

Figures such as **Mata Hari**, the famous dancer and spy of the First World War, or the cunning **Francis Walsingham**, spymaster of Queen Elizabeth I, have starred in episodes that mix suspense with reality. These espionage pioneers paved the way for the complex modern intelligence agencies we know today.

Another iconic episode illustrating the ingenuity and impact of intelligence in the 20th century takes us to Bletchley Park during the Second World War. Under the direction of **Alan Turing**, a group of mathematicians and cryptanalysts managed to decipher the codes of the **Enigma** machine, used by the Nazis. This milestone in cryptanalysis not only changed the course of the war, but also highlighted how technology became a driving force in the evolution of intelligence.

The proliferation of connected devices and the spread of digital platforms in the 21st century revolution have profoundly transformed society. This change has also redefined the landscape for security agencies, which have been forced to improve their ability to process colossal volumes of data. This context led to the emergence of the National Security Agency (NSA) in the United States, at a critical moment where the ethical and strategic dilemma of safeguarding the nation while respecting individual freedoms became palpable.

This new millennium introduces us to the revelations of **Edward Snowden**, who disclosed classified documents as an NSA contractor. These documents showed the dark side of massive electronic surveillance programs, raising crucial questions about the delicate balance between national safeguarding and individual rights.

The trajectory of intelligence agencies has aroused constant interest among those fascinated by these topics. Starting with the manual strategies of yesteryear to the digital age that characterizes our present, each stage has left an indelible mark on the way nations seek and use information for their security and protect their interests.

Each case analyzed represents a significant milestone in the culture of these organizations. The historical episodes highlight the great importance of adaptability and innovation in the field of intelligence over the centuries. The lessons learned whether at Bletchley Park decoding Enigma or in the revelation of electronic surveillance programs by Edward Snowden, underline the constant need to evolve and meet the changing challenges of the global environment.

Exploring this complex evolution not only connects us to the past, but also sheds light on the context in which intelligence agencies operate today. This journey reminds us of the importance of adaptability, innovation and ethics in a world where information is an invaluable asset and data is the new oil.

Value of intelligence: Data is the new oil

In an increasingly interconnected and dangerous world, understanding how intelligence agencies work is more important than ever. Its ability to **anticipate** and **prevent threats**, thus contributing to protecting national interests, is fundamental to the security and stability of all nations.

But its relevance goes beyond the circles of power and politics. Whether it's securing borders or protecting our online privacy, these agencies directly impact every person's daily life. Its ongoing work in the fight against organized crime, terrorism and other invisible threats, such as data theft, is essential to guarantee security and freedom in an increasingly complex and dangerous world.

Returning to the expression "data is the new oil", I invite you to take a brief break to enjoy a coffee or your favorite drink while I explain its meaning.

This comparison refers to the idea that, just as oil has been a source of wealth and power in the industrial age, data has similar value in the digital age. Data is abundant and generated in large quantities by individuals, businesses, and connected devices, giving it significant economic value.

Their strategic importance lies in the fact that they are essential to understanding market behavior, consumer trends and the internal operations of organizations. Like oil, data must be processed and analyzed to turn it into actionable information, which requires investments in data analytics technologies.

Furthermore, just as oil-rich countries have geopolitical influence, organizations and governments that control large amounts of data can exert power and control over the market and society. However, this raises concerns about privacy and ethical use of the information collected.

For this reason, intelligence agencies must operate with a **clear mission** and **specific defined objectives**, to avoid violations of rights, duplication of efforts, impersonation of functions, confusion of roles between agencies and waste of resources, which are always limited.

The mission of an intelligence agency is **multifaceted** and often addresses aspects crucial to national security. This may include the collection, analysis and dissemination of relevant information, as well as the protection of national interests.

Each State decides the role it assigns to its intelligence agencies. US agencies have their mission defined in the "**US National Security Directive**", a key document that assigns the National Security Agency (NSA) the responsibility of ensuring national security through the collection and analysis of intelligence information.

The specific objectives of an intelligence agency encompass a wide range of goals that contribute to the fulfillment of its mission. These may include **strategic information gathering**, **data analysis**, **threat prevention**, and national **decision-making advice**. And each of these objectives is a fundamental piece in the national security puzzle.

A widely recognized proposal, put forward by Mark M. Lowenthal in his book "Intelligence: From Secrets to Policy", defines the following basic objectives for a national intelligence agency:

- Provide accurate information and relevant knowledge.
- Evaluate and foresee possible future dangers.

- Preserve the security of citizens and the nation.
- Contribute to the formulation of national policies and strategies

In the modern era, these institutions must remain highly **adaptable**, as cyber challenges and threats, as well as geopolitical conditions, are **constantly changing**. The latent risk of information theft by state actors or terrorist groups requires a **prompt update** in terms of technology and intelligence strategies.

An example of a successful response to cyber threats is the *Olympic Games* Operation, in which the NSA, the Department of Defense and the CIA worked together to sabotage Iranian centrifuges, claiming that they were used in the production of enriched uranium for the manufacture of weapons nuclear.

An emblematic case of response to cyber threats related to the theft of information by state actors was the attack against the United States Office of Personnel Management (OPM) in 2014 and 2015. US authorities attributed damage to actors backed by the Chinese government, although China denied any involvement.

This was a sophisticated cyberattack that involved the theft of highly sensitive information, compromising the personal data of millions of federal employees, including personal background information and security clearance forms.

The incident generated a significant increase in the awareness of government officials about the need to allocate resources to strengthen cybersecurity measures, especially in institutions that handle extremely sensitive information.

It highlights the importance of international collaboration to address cyber threats, as well as the need for a proportional and strategic response. The OPM attack served as a critical reminder of the vulnerability of government institutions to cyber threats, and the response underscored the complexity of handling such incidents at the geopolitical and national security levels.

Evolution of key objectives over time

- **Strategic Gathering (Cold War):** During the Cold War, the CIA excelled at gathering strategic information, as evidenced by Venona Project, unraveling Soviet encrypted communications.
- **Effective Collaboration (Post 9/11):** After the attacks of September 11, 2001, intelligence agencies sought to improve collaboration to prevent future attacks, highlighting the need for adaptability.
- **Technological Innovation (Digital Age):** In the digital age, adaptation to emerging technologies and ethical data management have become crucial objectives for intelligence agencies.

The organizational structure of a national intelligence agency is a fundamental component that determines its effectiveness in the **collection**, **analysis** and **dissemination** of information critical to national security. By exploring it we gain a deeper insight into how these institutions manage and use information.

Detailing the **hierarchy** and internal **organization** of this type of agency is essential to understanding their roles, how they operate and how they carry out their functions, which are already complicated. But we won't give up! And in the following paragraphs, you will learn about some of the operational tactics that these structures implement to fulfill their mission and objectives.

The organizational structure of an intelligence agency can vary depending on the country and its specific focus, but generally follows a similar outline. Here I present a typical organizational structure of an intelligence agency:

1. **Management or senior leadership:**
    - Director or CEO: Top person in charge of

the agency, responsible for strategic decision making and general leadership.
- Deputy Director: Supports the director in his duties and replaces him in his absence.
- Advisory Board: May include external experts and advisors who provide strategic guidance.

2. **Operations Division:**
   - Foreign Intelligence: Compile information on activities and threats abroad.
   - Internal Intelligence: Focuses on the collection of information within the country itself.
   - Counterintelligence: Responsible for detecting and countering espionage activities against the agency.
   - Covert Operations: Conduct clandestine activities to gather information or carry out specific missions.
   - Analysis units: Process the collected information to produce useful intelligence.

3. **Technology and Support Division:**
   - Information technology: Manages the technological infrastructure necessary for data collection, storage and analysis.
   - Cybersecurity: Protects agency information systems against cyber threats.
   - Logistics support: Provides logistics and administration services to ensure the efficient operation of the agency.

4. **Human resources division:**
   - Recruitment and training: Responsible for recruiting and training new agents and analysts.
   - Staff Management: Manage existing staff, including task assignment and professional

development.
5. **Legal and ethics division:**
    - Legal advice: Provides legal advice on the agency's operations and ensures its compliance with national and international laws.
    - Ethics and Integrity: Monitors compliance with ethical standards and promotes integrity in all agency activities.
6. **Foreign relations and cooperation:**
    - Coordination with allied agencies: Facilitates collaboration and exchange of information with intelligence agencies of other countries.
    - Intelligence Diplomacy: Establishes relationships with foreign governments and international organizations to advance the agency's interests.

This structure provides an overview of how intelligence agencies are organized and function, but it is important to note that there can be significant variations depending on the context and specific needs of each agency and country. Furthermore, the exact structure can be classified based on information sensitivity and the need for compartmentalized knowledge. Remember that not everything that exists on this topic is published.

What almost all of us agree on is that we consider these agencies as fundamental pillars for the defense and protection of national interests around the world. His work goes beyond what is commonly known, entering a world of intrigue, analysis and covert action.

And now comes the funniest part! Because I want to invite you to take a look at the intriguing structures and security strategies of three titans of intelligence on a global scale: the **National Intelligence Directorate (DNI) of the United States**, the **Secret**

Service of Intelligence (MI6) of the **United Kingdom** and the secretive **Institute of Intelligence and Special Operations**, better known as **MOSSAD**, of **Israel.**

As a journalist and lawyer specialized in security, international relations, human rights and diplomacy, I am convinced that understanding the particularities and challenges of these agencies can be very useful for understanding this issue. That is why we will not limit ourselves to an "exploratory tourist" visit of the information they have on their website. Here we will attempt to distill the core of its existence to illuminate the nuances and contrasts that define its role in global security.

These three examples that I have selected for you are not just state entities with hidden agendas; They are microcosms of strategy, adaptation and constant challenge. The National Intelligence Directorate (DNI), MI6 and MOSSAD, each in its essence, reflects the delicate intersection between the **need to protect** and the **obligation to respect fundamental rights** on the complex game board of geopolitics.

Get ready to explore how the DNI, with its central role in the United States intelligence community, navigates the vast oceans of global information. Discover with me how MI6, with its distinguished tradition of espionage, impacts the UK's strategic decision-making. Learn from MOSSAD, whose shadow is projected on Israel's security, marking each movement in a volatile and conflictive geopolitical scenario.

So, grab a cup of your favorite coffee or beverage and join me on a tour of the complex structures and functions that make up the backbone of national security in three notable nations that you have surely visited or have on your upcoming travel list. Let's go!

1. United States - Directorate of National Intelligence (DNI):

The Directorate of National Intelligence (DNI) of the United States is a very particular agency, created to supervise and coordinate the activities of the 17 intelligence agencies of the United States Federal Government.

Established in 2005 under the Intelligence Reform and Terrorism Prevention Act, the DNI aims to integrate and unify the intelligence collection and analysis efforts of different agencies, such as the CIA, NSA and FBI, among others. Its role is to ensure that all these agencies effectively share information and coordinate their activities to protect the national security of the United States.

It operates with an organizational structure that reflects the complexity and breadth of its responsibilities. Its units and divisions are designed to address a variety of global challenges.

In the United States, the **highest authority of the Intelligence System is the President**. As Head of State and Commander in Chief of the Armed Forces, the President has the responsibility of leading and coordinating the intelligence community. Although the President is not directly in charge of all intelligence agencies, he has the authority to set priorities, receive key intelligence reports, and make strategic decisions based on information provided by these agencies.

The Director of National Intelligence (DNI) in the United States is the **central figure in the National Intelligence System (NIS)**. The Director of National Intelligence serves as the **President's principal** intelligence advisor and coordinates the work of the various intelligence agencies. However, final authority rests with the President, who has the capacity to give instructions and establish policy on matters of intelligence and national security.

In short, the DNI is the key figure that supervises and coordinates the operation of the National Intelligence System, advises the President and other key leaders on intelligence and national security issues. While managing the integration of information from various intelligence agencies, ensuring that it is shared and used effectively.

2. United Kingdom - Secret Intelligence Service (MI6):
Officially called *Secret Intelligence Service (SIS)*, MI6, founded in 1909, operates under the direction of the *Foreign Office* and headquarters are in Vauxhall Cross, London. It is the foreign intelligence agency responsible for collecting information on potential threats to the UK's national security, including terrorism, the proliferation of weapons of mass destruction and other geopolitical risks.

MI6 recruits and trains undercover agents, known as "spies", who carry out covert operations abroad to protect the UK's national interests.

Its hierarchical structure ensures efficient management of British intelligence. **The highest authority of the Intelligence System** is the **Prime Minister**, who has the responsibility of leading the Government and, therefore, plays a determining role in making decisions related to intelligence and national security.

The Prime Minister works closely with various intelligence agencies, MI6 being one of them. In addition, the United Kingdom's National Security Council, chaired by the Prime Minister, plays an important role in formulating security policy and coordinating intelligence-related matters.

It is critical to note that the UK has a complex structure of intelligence agencies, and decision-making can involve multiple levels and government actors. However, ultimate authority lies with the political leadership, specifically the Prime Minister.

The Head of the MI6 Service in the United Kingdom is the highest authority of this intelligence agency. Although there is no official title of "Head of Service" in the legislation governing MI6, it is generally the term used to refer to the agency's leader.

The Head of Service's relationship with the British intelligence system involves **coordination and collaboration** with other intelligence agencies, with **MI5 (Security Service)** being the sister agency of MI6. Both services work together to address national security threats, both internal and external.

In addition, MI6 works closely with other components of the British intelligence system, such as the Government Communications Center (GCHQ) and the Military Intelligence Service (MI1 and MI2), to collect and analyze information of interest. strategic.

In simple terms, the relationship involves effective coordination between the various British intelligence agencies to ensure national security and address threats comprehensively.

3. Israel - Intelligence and Special Operations Institute (MOSSAD, acronym in Hebrew):

Mossad, as the Israeli intelligence agency is more commonly known, is one of the most prestigious and secretive intelligence agencies in the world. Founded in 1949, it has primary responsibility for gathering information, conducting covert operations, and conducting counterterrorism activities on behalf of Israel.

The agency operates both inside and outside Israel, using a network of undercover agents, foreign intelligence stations and collaborators in different parts of the world. It has earned a reputation for efficiency and boldness in its operations, using innovative methods and cutting-edge technology to achieve its objectives.

Its focus on human intelligence and special operations stands out in its adaptability, because it engages in a wide range of activities, including military intelligence, counterintelligence, combating terrorism, infiltration of hostile groups, gathering threat information. external and internal, and the protection of Israeli citizens abroad.

In the context of **Israel's National Intelligence System**, the

highest authority is the Prime Minister. The Prime Minister has a key role in making decisions related to intelligence and national security. He is the political leader and has the responsibility of directing and coordinating intelligence operations in the country.

The Prime Minister works closely with other leaders and intelligence agencies, including the Director of Mossad and other key officials. The intelligence decision-making structure is designed to be a comprehensive process, where political leadership plays a central role.

It is important to note that the exact structure and responsibilities may vary, and intelligence decisions may also involve the National Security Council and other government agencies. However, the figure of the Prime Minister represents the highest political authority in Israel and plays a crucial role in intelligence and national security matters.

The **Mossad Director's hierarchical relationship** with Israel's National Intelligence System reflects a structure of **coordination and cooperation**. The Israeli National Intelligence System is designed to integrate and coordinate the activities of the different intelligence agencies in the country, including the Mossad.

Although each intelligence agency, including Mossad, has independent leadership, there is a framework for collaboration and joint work within the National Intelligence System. Cooperation between agencies is essential to address security threats comprehensively and efficiently.

The Mossad Director is an integral part of this structure, collaborating with other intelligence leaders to exchange information, assess threats, and coordinate actions when necessary. While the Director of Mossad leads agency-specific operations, he works in concert with the leadership of the National Intelligence System to ensure a unified response to security challenges.

Simply put, the hierarchical relationship implies that the Mossad Director, while leading his own agency, operates in a broader environment of collaboration and coordination within Israel's National Intelligence System.

These agencies, with their complex structures and appointed leaders, play a vital role in protecting national security, each weaving its own narrative into the web of global intelligence.

If you still have some doubts, and I suppose you do, about the organizational structures of these emblematic agencies, I suggest you take a break from your routine. Follow my advice and this weekend or on your next break, lose yourself in the intriguing world of **"Espionage Missions"** available on Netflix. From the machinations of MI6 to the covert operations of the CIA, this documentary reveals fascinating facts about the art of spying, Cold War campaigns and coups carried out by secret agents.

Books / movies and series - 60 key facts
[The World of Intelligence Agencies]

BOOKS:

1. ***"The Secret World: A History of Intelligence"*** - Christopher Andrew, 2019

The book "The Secret World: A History of Intelligence" is a milestone in the global historical study of espionage. From biblical times to the modern era, Andrew guides us through the mysteries of the world of intelligence in a fascinating journey. This 960-page work recovers much of the lost history of intelligence over the past three millennia, highlighting its continued relevance in our times.

In its pages, the secrets and operations of spies over the centuries are revealed, offering a unique vision of how intelligence has evolved and influenced world events. From the intriguing tales of ancient times to the sophisticated methods of the modern era, this book reveals the complexities and mysteries of the world of espionage.

With unexpected comparisons and a captivating narrative, it invites the reader to immerse themselves in the intriguing history of intelligence. If you are interested in learning more about the exciting world of espionage, this work is essential for you. Available on Amazon https://amzn.to/4afRFjx

2. ***"Intelligence: From Secrets to Policy"*** - Mark M. Lowenthal, 2019

The book "Intelligence: From Secrets to Policy", written by Lowenthal, is an essential guide to understanding how the history, structure, procedures and functions of the intelligence community affect political decisions. Throughout its 616 pages, Lowenthal demystifies a complex process and offers a clear and accessible vision of how intelligence influences global political decisions.

In its fully updated eighth edition, Lowenthal addresses topics such as cybersecurity and cyber intelligence. In addition, it expands the coverage of information collection and comprehensively updates the chapters on national affairs and transnational problems. It also examines foreign intelligence services, both large and small, from the Cold War to current challenges.

With a captivating narrative and deep analysis, it invites the reader to immerse themselves in the fascinating history of intelligence and its role in global politics. This text is essential reading to gain an in-depth understanding of the intriguing world of espionage. Available on Googlebooks https://books.google.com.do/books?id=Fk6YDwAAQBAJ

3. *"The Orange Seller"* - Blanca Miosi, 2021

This novel by Blanca Miosi, one of the most audacious authors of Latin American literature, presents a plot that involves several intelligence agencies. The protagonist, Ramón Latorre de los Cobos y Ugarte, during his stay in England, becomes a member of World Without Communism or WWC. There, he has his first meeting with Peter Beigent, an observer for the Secret Intelligence Service, better known as MI6 or SIS.

After graduating in International Law from the University of Cambridge, Ramón returns to Spain and takes the reins of the family orange business. Shortly after, he receives a call from Peter Beigent to carry out a task that only an orange seller can perform.

Throughout the novel, intelligence agencies play a crucial role in the plot, as Ramón faces the challenges of espionage and international politics, becoming a key player in the future of the world during the Cold War, from the end of the Spanish Civil War until the fall of the Soviet Union. His life becomes involved in a series of intrigues that include falling in love with a Russian spy, with consequences that will affect the rest of his life. Available on Amazon https://amzn.to/43WFs1a

4. *"The Spy"* - A Espiã | Paulo Coelho, 2017

In the novel "The Spy: The Life of Mata Hari" Paulo Coelho transports us to an interesting version of the famous exotic dancer and courtesan who challenged the conventions of Europe at the beginning of the 20th century. Through a series of letters between Mata Hari and her lawyer, Coelho offers us an intimate portrait of this enigmatic woman as she awaits the verdict in her trial for alleged espionage for France and Germany.

From exotic Java to the vibrant Paris of the Belle Époque and Berlin in the midst of World War I, Mata Hari defended her dreams and lived her life to the fullest, guided by the words her mother repeated to her in her childhood: "To the trees taller ones come from small seeds". With her sensuality, strength and contradictions, she stands as an icon of the fight for independence and freedom in a constantly changing world.

If you are curious about the fascinating role played by many women as spies, this work "The Spy: The Life of Mata Hari" by Paulo Coelho is an exceptional choice. Available https://amzn.to/3PFEiko

5. *"Spy School"* - Stuart Gibbs, 2020

In "Spy School" a series of exciting novels for young people and adults, written by Stuart Gibbs. We discover Ben Ripley, a 12-year-old boy who, under the guise of a scholarship to a science school, is admitted to a covert institution that trains future junior CIA agents.

From the first moment, Ben is immersed in the complex world of espionage, full of dangers, false identities and double games. The "Spy School" series consists of 10 books that narrate the exciting adventures of young spies in training. The titles are: "Spy School", "Spy Camp", "Evil Spy School", "Spy Ski School", "Spy School Secret Service", "Spy School Goes South", "Spy School British Invasion", "Spy School Revolution", "Spy School at Sea" and "Spy School Project

Each book features exciting missions and challenges that characters must overcome on their path to becoming top-level secret agents. If you are fluent in both English and Spanish, I highly recommend reading the entire series! Available on Amazon https://amzn.to/3PLHWcO_and the complete series https://amzn.to/3IZTAgo

FILMS:

1. **"Shepherd"** – (USA, 2006)

[Espionage]

"Shepherd", also known as "The Good Shepherd", is an American thriller directed by Robert De Niro and starring Robert De Niro, Matt Damon and Angelina Jolie. The film delves into the early years of the CIA and counterintelligence, exploring the complex world of espionage through historical events such as the failed Bay of Pigs invasion in 1961. Through the life of the main character, Edward Wilson, Based in part on Cold War counterintelligence chief James Angleton, the film reveals the personal and moral cost of intelligence work, highlighting the sacrifices, deception and betrayal it involves. Although the film takes artistic liberties, it offers valuable lessons on the history of espionage, ethical dilemmas, and the importance of internal security in modern intelligence agencies. It is important to remember that although it is a work of fiction, "The Good Shepherd" can spark meaningful discussions about ethics and morality in the world of spies. Enjoy it on Movistar Plus, Apple TV and Filmin, also depending on your region, you could find it for free on other platforms such as Tubi or YouTube.

2. **"The Catcher Was a Spy"** – (USA, 2018)

[Undercover agent]

"The Catcher Was a Spy", based on true events, tells the life of Moe Berg, a professional baseball player turned spy during World War II. Played by Paul Rudd, Berg offers a unique perspective to the world of espionage, highlighting the importance of his linguistic and intellectual skills to the United States Office of Strategic Services. The plot, which includes evaluation of German progress on the atomic bomb and ethical decisions on the ground, highlights the need for diverse skills and scientific intelligence in recruiting agents. Additionally, it underscores the importance of interagency and international work and explores the personal cost of espionage, offering valuable lessons for modern intelligence agencies on ethics, collaboration, and the personal well-being of their agents. It is available on Amazon Prime Video.

3. **"Munich"** – (USA, 2005)

[Covert Operations - MOSSAD]

"Munich", directed by Steven Spielberg, is an intense historical drama that addresses real events, based on the book "Vengeance" by George Jonas. The plot follows a MOSSAD commando tasked with avenging the 1972 Munich Olympics massacre, carrying out operations to eliminate the Palestinians responsible. The film, starring Eric Bana, Daniel Craig and Ciarán Hinds, explores the complex personal and ethical repercussions of engaging in secret missions of revenge and espionage in a dangerous world. Although the film takes certain artistic liberties, it offers several lessons for decision-makers on intelligence issues, including the planning of covert operations, ethical and moral dilemmas, agent safety, and the political and diplomatic consequences of intelligence actions. Find it on platforms like Apple TV,

Movistar Plus, Rakuten TV or Google TV.

4. **"Spy Game"** – (USA, 2001)

[Loyalty and betrayal]

"Spy Game" is a thrilling espionage thriller that centers on Nathan Muir, an experienced CIA agent, and his protégé Tom Bishop. Set in 1991, the day of Muir's retirement, the plot thickens when he learns that Bishop is imprisoned in China, accused of espionage and facing the death penalty within 24 hours. To save his disciple, he is forced to act outside the CIA and find a way to free him. The film, starring Robert Redford and Brad Pitt, offers memorable dialogue that explores the nature of espionage and loyalty. Although a work of fiction, it allows for valuable learnings about mentoring and training, covert operations, sacrifice and loyalty, manipulation and deception, as well as the challenges of retiring and adapting to civilian life, which are relevant to modern intelligence agencies, highlighting the importance of preparation, strategy, ethics and adaptability in the world of espionage. Depending on your location, it will be available on Amazon Prime Video, Filmin, Movistar Plus and Tivify.

5. **"The Spy Next Door"** – (USA, 2010)

[Emotional vulnerability]

"The Spy Next Door", starring Jackie Chan, is a family action comedy that, while primarily intended to entertain, also offers some interesting lessons that are useful to consider. The plot follows Bob Ho, an undercover CIA agent, who, living with his girlfriend and three children, finds himself involved in an unexpected and challenging situation when he must balance his life as a spy with his responsibility as a babysitter while facing terrorists. Russians. The film raises awareness about the efficient and intelligent use of technology for surveillance and personal security, as well as the need to maintain a healthy balance between professional and personal life. In addition, it highlights the importance of teamwork, adaptability and the use of resources in unexpected situations. This type of film can serve as exercises or dynamics to discuss values such as the importance of family, honesty, and the consequences of using violence to resolve conflicts. Although it is a comedy, it offers an interesting perspective on the world of espionage and its possible lessons. You can enjoy it as a family or as a team, on Amazon Prime Video and Movistar Plus.

SERIES:

1. **"The Looming Tower"** – (USA, 2018)

[10 Episodes | 1 Season]

"The Looming Tower" is a drama series based on the Pulitzer Prize-winning book, "The Looming Tower", written by Lawrence Wright. The plot explores the confrontation between the FBI and the CIA in the 90s as they tried to prevent Al-Qaeda attacks. This production reveals the tension and lack of coordination that often occurs between these intelligence agencies, offering a fascinating portrait of the events that triggered the 9/11 attacks, as well as the subsequent war in Afghanistan and its lasting consequences.

Starring Jeff Daniels, Tahar Rahim and Alec Baldwin, "The Looming Tower" premiered in the United States on Hulu in February 2018 and was later available worldwide on other platforms such as Amazon Prime Video. If you are interested in the history of North American intelligence and the events that marked the beginning of the 21st century, this proposal is an unmissable option for you.

2. **"The Bureau"** - Le Bureau des Légendes – (FRA, 2015)

[50 Episodes | 5 Seasons]

"The Bureau", which occupies first place in the Ranking of "Best French series of all time", is based on real stories of ex-spies, inspired by contemporary events and revolves around the daily life and missions of the agents of the DGSE (General Directorate of External Security) in areas of French interest around the world, living under false identities for years, to identify and recruit good intelligence sources.

In "The Bureau", intelligence officer Guillaume Debailly, codenamed "Malotru" (literally "churl"), after six years of infiltration in Damascus, returns to Paris and faces the challenge of reconnecting with his daughter, his ex-wife, his colleagues and even his former self. However, his return to "normal life" proves complicated, especially when he discovers that Nadia, his love in Damascus, is also in Paris. This successful production quickly reached the top ratings on iTunes with the international label "Episodic Cinema" and since June 2016 it was acquired for the exclusive Amazon Prime billboard. If you are curious about the world of espionage and the challenges that agents face in their work, "The Bureau" is a different option that will captivate you from beginning to end.

3. **"Spooks"** - Military Intelligence 5 "MI-5" – (UK, 2015)
[86 Episodes | 10 Seasons]

"Spooks", also known as "MI-5", is a multi-BAFTA award-winning British drama series. It follows a group of MI5 intelligence officers, known as " The Grid ", as they carry out missions inside the United Kingdom, facing terrorist threats and internal conspiracies. The series explores the ethical and emotional implications of MI-5 operations, as well as the challenges the agents face when balancing their professional lives with their personal relationships and their loyalty to the country, including high-level negotiations and power struggles.

"Spooks" features the advanced technology used by MI-5, including electronic surveillance and computer hacking. In addition, it reveals betrayals within the agency and delves into the personal relationships of the agents, adding complexity to the characters. It was released on iTunes for viewers in the United States and Canada, but all seasons of "Spooks" are also available on Amazon Prime Video. By the way, in 2015 the movie "Spooks: The Greater Good" as a continuation of the series.

4. **"Alias"** – (USA, 2001)

[105 Episodes | 5 Seasons]

"Alias" tells the story of Sydney Bristow, an intelligent and athletic young woman recruited by SD-6, a secret branch of a large criminal organization that, under the guise of a secret division of the CIA, carries out illicit financial operations. Discovering the deception, Sydney seeks help from the real CIA, where she becomes a double agent to dismantle the SD-6 structure.

The series follows Sydney on her undercover missions around the world, facing off against deadly enemies, solving family mysteries, and struggling to keep her double life a secret. "Alias" is recognized for its intrigue, action and unexpected twists, as well as the development of complex interpersonal relationships. Throughout its five seasons, it will surprise you with an exciting mix of espionage, drama and suspense, illustrating how these agencies can affect even the lives of ordinary people. All its episodes are on Amazon Prime Video, JustWatch and Disney Plus.

5. **"The Americans"** – (USA, 2013)

[75 Episodes | 6 Seasons]

"The Americans", winner of an Emmy and a Golden Globe. It is set in the 80s during Ronald Reagan's administration, a tense period between the United States and the Soviet Union. The story is about a couple of Soviet spies trained and infiltrated as American citizens.

These spies from the Committee for State Security or KGB have lived the last fifteen years on the outskirts of Washington DC as a supposed married couple, with two children who are unaware of this double life. Their secret operations are put at risk after the death of one of their officers and the arrival in the neighborhood of an FBI agent specializing in counterintelligence, who maintains a tense relationship with his wife due to work. If you are passionate about the world of espionage and the challenges that agents face in their work, you will love this television series and its meticulous construction of ambiguous decisions. You can find it on Amazon Prime Video, Disney Plus, StarPlus and other portals.

In this chapter, we have embarked on a journey to the heart of intelligence agencies, exploring their **definition**, **function** and **evolution** throughout history, as well as their **importance** in the current global context.

From gathering information to protecting national interests, its agents work tirelessly to ensure security in a complex and dynamic world. The cases I have mentioned to you, including examples with books, movies and series, illustrate how these organizations and the staff who work for them face challenges while pursuing their objectives. Whether in spy operations in the Cold War or in response to cyber threats affecting banking systems today, they continue to play a vital role in national security.

Through changing times and challenges, these institutions have persevered, maintained, adapted and evolved to fulfill their commitment to the collective security of each of their countries.

But this is just the beginning. Throughout this book, we will continue this mission to discover the 60 key facts that will reveal the truth behind intelligence agencies and the impact of their operations on our daily lives.

Before moving on to the next chapter, I suggest you choose a movie or series that I have selected to recommend to you. Now, with the knowledge you already have about the world of spies, you can be a critical viewer and learn more about this fascinating topic while enjoying the proposals of the seventh art.

Prepare the popcorn and join the conversation! Discuss with friends and colleagues about topics that arise. If you share your moments on social media, or have any other comments about the book, tag me on @mujerseguridad and tell me who won the award for the best popcorn.

CHAPTER 2: THE PILLARS OF INTELLIGENCE

Intelligence agencies are multifaceted organizations, whose functions, operations and methods differ considerably from traditional State institutions. Their work transcends conventional limits, as they are constantly adapting and facing the changing challenges of the global environment.

Although these organizations have certain "special powers", their operation is strictly regulated by laws and other regulations. They must always operate within a legal framework that establishes clear limits and control mechanisms to ensure transparency in the efficient use of resources and compliance with the law and ethical principles.

The size and structure of each intelligence agency is unique and designed to adapt to the specific needs, challenges and capabilities of its home country. However, its work will always be based on three fundamental pillars: **information collection**, **data analysis** and **intelligence generation**.

Let's start with the first one: **information gathering**. This phase involves the active and passive search for data, from open sources to classified sources, with the aim of obtaining a complete and accurate view of the situation at hand.

Once the information is collected, we enter the second pillar:

data analysis. This is where experts thoroughly examine everything collected, identifying patterns, trends, and potential threats. This process requires strong analytical skills and the use of advanced tools to extract meaningful insights from the flood of available material.

Finally, we arrive at the third pillar: **the generation of intelligence.** At this stage, analysts transform operational data and resources, filtering only information relevant to the intended purpose, providing decision makers with critical information to address national security challenges and protect the country's interests. This intelligence comes in various formats, such as strategic reports and threat assessments, but plays a vital role in policy and strategy formulation.

From the collection to the analysis and dissemination of information, these organizations play a role that transcends what is commonly highlighted in news headlines. In this chapter, I want to show you in greater detail the essential foundations that underpin the work of intelligence agencies, and that influence government decision-making at a national and international level, their contribution to the protection of society as a whole, and how Their work impacts the daily lives of people like you and me.

Fundamental pillars of intelligence

When you hear in the news about the dismantling of a drug trafficking network, child prostitution or the prevention of a terrorist attack, this does not happen "by magic" or "by pure chance"; It is the result of hard work monitoring and collecting key data that allows authorities to act preventively. These actions may seem distant from our daily lives, but in fact, they are decisive in keeping us safe and protected.

The role of intelligence agencies in your daily routine is fundamental, but if they do their job well, you should not know about it. The greatest success of a spy is to go unnoticed.

Its function is to provide critical information that contributes to protecting the security and well-being of the nation, in multiple aspects, ranging from the prevention of crimes to the anticipation of international crises.

The spies, or agents, as they are called now, but they continue doing the same thing. They are dedicated to bringing together scattered pieces of information that circulate around the world, with the aim of forming a complete and understandable picture. This involves intercepting communications, collecting data from human sources, and monitoring various sources of information.

Once the information is collected, the next step is to carefully analyze it to extract meaningful insights and discern patterns, trends and potential threats on a national and international scale.

For example, if an increase in suspicious cyber activity is identified, agencies can alert authorities and the general public about potential digital security threats. In this process they will use advanced technological tools and techniques to determine patterns, detect potential threats and predict future trends. This can lead to increased awareness and adoption of preventive measures by citizens and businesses to protect themselves against potential cyber-attacks.

These basic functions – **collection**, **analysis** and **dissemination** – form a trilogy that defines the daily work of Intelligence Agencies at a global level. As directors of an information orchestra, these agencies not only monitor, interpret and share data, but also shape national security and strategic decision-making in each of our countries.

In the following sections, we will further explore the methods and secrets of operations, official portals to obtain some of these technological tools for free, revealing aspects that were previously reserved for expert personnel versed in the arts of espionage and intelligence.

Information gathering

On any given day, you wake up, check your mobile phone to check the news, listen to the radio while you go to work or school, and perhaps take advantage of a break to check your social networks. In each of these moments, you interact with sources of information that are collected, analyzed and shared at some level by your country's secret intelligence and security services.

One of the oldest and most effective ways to collect information is through human sources. These can be spies, undercover agents, informants or simply ordinary citizens who, voluntarily or inadvertently, provide valuable data. For example, every post you share on your social networks can become a data point for **open- source intelligence,** a concept I'll explain later.

Even that friend who presumes to know everything that happens in the neighborhood could be being used as **an inadvertent informant,** thus facilitating the work of intelligence organizations. Remember that human connections are used by security services to inform themselves about potential threats, criminal activities or relevant geopolitical changes. In this sense, the informant is a highly valued resource for several fundamental reasons.

These individuals provide privileged access to information that may be difficult to obtain otherwise, offering timely data. Additionally, the diversity of sources they represent allows you to obtain a more complete picture of the situation, validate data, and develop relationships with key figures in various settings.

There are countless types of informants, but the most common classifications include **paid informants,** who receive compensation for their collaboration; the **unpaid,** who share information voluntarily; the **inadvertent,** who provide data without realizing their role; collaborators, who cooperate under formal agreements for legal benefits or other interests; the **coverts,** who infiltrate groups to obtain information from within; and others, depending on the context and the specific criteria of each situation.

At the core of intelligence gathering lies an ancient art: **human espionage.** This world is populated by shadowy and discreet figures who become crucial actors on the information stage. It is astonishing to watch how these spies or secret agents operate, often without receiving recognition for the sacrifices they make, not even by their own families, for the security and stability of the nation.

Many of them work under false identities, trusting in the discretion of government leaders and intelligence services. It must also be recognized that it requires extraordinary talent to assume other people's identities and hide their true intentions. Not everyone develops the skills that are essential in this dangerous profession, of being a spy, which no State has been able to do without.

Espionage is a clandestine activity, as we already know, through which a person, usually representing a government or organization, collects confidential or secret information from another entity without its knowledge or consent. Its objectives can range from military, political, economic, scientific to technological data, among others. Spies usually operate in absolute secrecy, employing various tactics ranging from the use of listening devices to infiltrating target organizations or recruiting human sources. However, the discovery of such activities could entail important legal and diplomatic implications, in addition to the permanent risk of the spy's death, as has happened in countless cases.

The origin of espionage dates back to ancient times, being an activity that has existed throughout the history of humanity. The first forms of clandestine research can be found in ancient civilizations such as the Egyptian, Chinese, Greek, Hebrew and Roman, where various techniques were used to obtain clues about enemies, their military movements and political plans.

In ancient China, for example, they used spies to obtain information about military strategies and enemy intentions. Sun Tzu, author of "The Art of War", wrote extensively about the importance of intelligence and espionage in military victory.

Historians report that, in Rome, soldiers were sent as scouts to infiltrate enemy territory and collect even the smallest details about their forces and secret plans. During the Middle Ages, European monarchs used spies to learn about the movements of their rivals and protect their political and territorial interests. Over time, this dangerous but exciting profession has developed and evolved, adapting to technological advances and changing according to geopolitical dynamics.

Author Carmen Posadas, who describes herself as a spy by vocation, addresses in her book **"License to Spy"** the peculiar and picturesque way in which the German Spy Museum in Berlin presents the visitor with the concept that espionage is the second oldest profession in the world, preceded only by prostitution. Or perhaps the oldest, if we take into account that, since the dawn of humanity, to survive it has been essential to inform ourselves about what rival or enemy tribes were doing.

Carmen also assures that the majority of scholars of this phenomenon agree in pointing out that, in the Western world, the oldest documented mention of the **action of spies** appears in the book of Numbers, chapter 13, where Moses sends twelve spies, one of each tribe of Israel, to explore the land of Canaan, collect information about its people and its strengths, to report to Moses, before the entry of the people of Israel into it. An espionage mission that was so unsuccessful that it is still used as an object of study in CIA and MOSSAD training.

But the concept "spy" already appears four times before in the sacred text, in the ancient book of Genesis, in chapter 42, where Joseph, sold by his own brothers as a slave and arrived in Egypt, becomes an influential figure in Pharaoh's court.

In Genesis 42:9, Joseph recognizes his brothers in Egypt during the famine and accuses them of being spies, suggesting that they are there to assess the country's weakness. In verse 42:12, he reiterates his accusation, and after questioning them in 42:14, Joseph maintains his suspicions. Finally, in verse 42:16, he leaves them detained in Egypt under the accusation of being spies, until one of them travels to Canaan to bring his younger brother, Benjamin. This biblical account illustrates the ancient and dramatic use of espionage, with Joseph playing a crucial role in intrigue and confrontation.

The theme of espionage is present in several biblical stories. In the God Speaks Today version, 32 verses refer to intriguing episodes or illustrate the use of intelligence in secret missions to achieve divine and earthly objectives. Iconic characters such as Joseph, Moses, Joshua, Rahab, David, Job, Samson, Judas and Jesus are involved in these stories.

According to the accounts of Mark and Luke, the scribes and Pharisees established a spy service specialized in monitoring the activities of Jesus of Nazareth. These teachers of the law infiltrated spies or "undercover agents", that nice name they call them now, to gather evidence that would allow them to subject him under the jurisdiction of the Roman governor.

Today, espionage continues to play a critical role in politics, national security and also in the business world, with intelligence agencies and security services around the globe dedicated to **collecting** any data of interest and **analyzing** alerts about potential threats and adversary activities.

In this mirror universe, real spies don't always have the charm of James Bond or the skills of Mr. and Mrs. Smith. Rarely are their days so extravagant, usually **secret agents** hide among us, with everyday roles and unattractive routines, which are far from the crucial missions they are executing. For example: Imagine your Uber taxi driver. Maybe it's not just taking you from one place to another, it could be collecting relevant details from someone of interest on the streets of the city? Now let's think about your favorite waiter, you love his courtesy, disposition and agility. But perhaps by serving dishes and waiting tables, he discreetly collects data crucial to the country's defense, at best. Do you have any idea what intelligence information is worth to a competing company? Not to mention other examples, outside the law, which are not the subject of this book.

Even your hairdresser, with her deft hands and pleasant conversation, could be listening more than she lets on, capturing snippets of conversations that might be of interest to the intelligence service. Even the parker who receives your car keys could be more connected than you imagine, watching and listening while he works in the shadows.

The ability to blend in with everyday tasks is essential for the success of these operations. Spies must be able to fully integrate into their environments, establish credible relationships, and perform their tasks without raising suspicion. This requires specialized training in infiltration techniques, covert communication, and handling false identities.

These secret operatives or agents, camouflaged in ordinary activities, stealthily play a vital role in delicate missions, for the benefit of their nation, aware that they will not be able to have public recognition for the success achieved. Have you stopped to think about it before?

With that idea in mind, I propose a coffee break. Find your cup, or the drink you prefer. And while we enjoy it, let's let our imagination fly with some everyday roles that could hide spies or "secret agents", or any of those interesting names they call you now:

- **The personal trainer:** At the gym or anywhere else, this individual not only helps his clients achieve their fitness goals but is also attentive to useful details that may arise during conversations or exercise sessions.

- **The traveling artist:** Visualize a street artist who, while painting urban landscapes, is discreetly observing and listening around to him, capturing key conversations between passersby.

- **The food delivery person:** In the era of home delivery, a food delivery person has access to different neighborhoods and homes, which gives him the opportunity to collect sensitive information while delivering your order, and mine too. who knows?

- **The pet sitter:** In your visits to different homes to care for animals, you can be a discreet observer of people's daily lives, taking the opportunity to collect relevant data and much more.

- **The street musician:** He entertains passersby with his musical talent, without distracting from his interesting mission, listening and observing behavior in the public. While you and I innocently enjoy their show.

- **The language teacher:** This character works with students from different countries. An ideal activity to obtain crucial details about international events and cultural trends. In an environment of trust, you engage in conversations that allow you to discreetly collect data. He can also indoctrinate and recruit followers to achieve his objectives.

- **The event planner:** Leverages his access to a wide range of exclusive people and places to blatantly spy on his target, dissembling with his social skills while discreetly collecting sensitive data at parties and gatherings without raising suspicion.

- **The observant nanny:** She really takes care of the children of a family and guarantees their safety, but she also extracts information from them, with her sweet interrogations, such as: and what did dad do last night? Did he bring money? Or did he hit mom? And it doesn't stop there, he also applies his innocent interrogation to other parents in parks, schools and extracurricular activities. And it applies the same pattern to the entire environment of its target.

- **The discreet butler:** Manages relevant data on routines and patterns of domestic behaviors of persons of interest; You can also keep an eye on guest conversations and collect relevant details during events and dinners.

- **The personal assistant:** Works for a high-level personality; Not only does he organize his agenda, but he may also be responsible for keeping up to date with his boss's movements and plans, providing reports to the agency, without raising suspicions.

- **Infiltrated cleaning:** A cleaning staff in a company or office can move discreetly through the facilities, observing and listening to important conversations between employees, managers or clients, thus obtaining privileged knowledge.

- **The confidential chauffeur:** A personal driver who transports executives, businessmen or politicians can witness confidential conversations in the car. Additionally, you know the private routines and behaviors of those personalities. You are ideally positioned to gather essential data on your target and report it to the intelligence agency.

- **The undercover chef:** She works for high-profile figures, but in addition to preparing exquisite meals, her mission is to be aware of situations of interest and important conversations between diners, to achieve her goal.

- **The observer gardener:** With access to private outdoor areas, you can use your position to observe and listen to residents and their visitors. His screen work allows him to verify places, confirm suspicions and report the daily routine of his target.

- **The confidential therapist:** Your massage therapist or personal care therapist could learn a lot about their clients' habits, routines, and relationships, providing unique insight that could be of interest to intelligence agencies. In these places, people feel comfortable and begin to chat and share compromising personal and professional details, without realizing that their therapist is spying on them, collecting relevant resources for their research.

- **The discreet accountant:** With privileged and confidential access to the financial situation of his target. While managing your clients' finances, you can detect financial patterns, unusual transactions or suspicious activities that could indicate illicit activities or hidden interests, without arousing suspicion of the person you work for.

- **The intrepid technician:** While repairing security cameras, alarm systems or electronic locks, you can access restricted areas and observe or capture private data without raising suspicion. The worst thing is that you can install your camouflaged listening or recording devices on the security devices you repaired. It is very common for covert or clandestine collection.

- **The curious "handyman":** This multitasking spy performs repairs around the home or office, and is generally very helpful and collaborative. While repairing this and that he is not distracted from his true mission, to observe, discreetly listen to conversations between residents or employees and collect relevant information that may be in plain sight. Sometimes you can place microphones or other covert surveillance equipment in strategic places you would never imagine.

- **The scheming lover:** This charming person who provides company on the lonely nights of influential people or political leaders. Does it look familiar to you? However, behind that facade of passion and romance, he could be playing a much darker role. Her charm and abilities to manipulate emotions make her a powerful instrument in the intelligence gathering arsenal. This type of spy is capable of accessing intimate secrets and key decisions, which is why this figure has influenced the course of history over time.

- **The unnoticed homeless person:** In the bustling streets of the city, among the darkest and most forgotten corners, this individual goes unnoticed by most, but his senses are always attentive. He becomes a silent witness to secret conversations, suspicious exchanges and strategic moves, capable of unearthing secrets hidden in the most unexpected places.

- **The health assistant:** With his discretion and accessibility, he listens to conversations between doctors and patients, picks up whispers in the hallways and observes the movements of suspicious visitors to gather vital details about the health status of influential people, the medical plans of emergency and other medical secrets that could even affect national security.

- **The garbage collector:** His discreet presence and access to restricted areas allows him to collect evidence about gang activity, drug trafficking, household and organizational consumption patterns, and even the planning of terrorist activities. With his apparent insignificance, the garbage collector becomes an unnoticed spy on the city streets, playing a crucial role in public safety.

- **The kindergarten teacher:** With her tenderness and cunning, as a confidant of the little ones, she obtains essential information about their families, their environment and their daily experiences. She becomes a guardian, who also indoctrinates them, protecting the future of the nation from the classrooms of the little ones.

- **The caregiver of older adults:** By listening to the life stories of the elderly and observing the details of their environment, she accumulates important data about her patient, family and social dynamics, and any other private details that may be of interest to her superiors. Every gesture, every word, is carefully recorded in her mind like pieces of a puzzle she is assembling.

- **The undercover prostitute:** This clandestine figure moves in the shadows, with people from all walks of life, from politicians and businessmen to artists and public officials. While satisfying the desires and fantasies of her clients, she collects scattered pieces of information, which she then skillfully puts together into a puzzle of strategic knowledge. With her bravery and wit, she becomes a key player in the complicated game of intelligence, where seduction and deception are weapons as powerful as the truth itself.

- **The simulated lady-in-waiting:** In elitist circles and luxurious residences, this enigmatic figure engages in refined conversations and listens attentively to her clients' confidences. This beautiful spy collects essential data on high society intrigues, family secrets and political alliances. Her ability to read between the lines and detect the most subtle gestures makes her a perceptive observer, capable of discovering hidden truths behind the most sophisticated appearances. Through her discreet presence in salons and exclusive parties, with her grace and cunning, she stands as a key piece in the complex network of intelligence, where elegance and discretion are as important as determination and courage.

The list of the jobs of spies or secret agents is truly fascinating and could be extended indefinitely, offering a unique vision of the mimicry capacity of these mysterious characters. However, due to limitations of time, space and resources, it is necessary to stop here.

Before concluding, I would like to share with you the icing on the cake. Sometimes agencies decide to add an additional layer of complexity and emotional tension to the context of human espionage by involving family members. This can create a conflict between family loyalty and the professional duty to fulfill the mission. Here are some examples:

• **The informant brother:** When an agency recruits someone who works at a company important to national security, it often thinks about involving his brother, sister or another close person to protect him. Thanks to his access to sensitive information, this brother can become an undercover spy, being the unwitting messenger who passes secret data to the intelligence agency.

• **The infiltrated father or mother:** If a public official is of interest to an intelligence agency, his or her children can be recruited and become domestic spies to report on the actions of their parent. They are also an ideal way to discreetly pass important information when the official collaborates with the agency.

• **The covert romantic partner:** When the partner of an

influential person in politics or business is recruited as a covert agent, they become an interesting resource for the intelligence agency. By having access to confidential information and private conversations, you can collect relevant data and discreetly transmit it to the agency. This intimate relationship and trust between the couple are key elements that facilitate obtaining security-relevant data.

- **The observing nephew or godson:** A nephew or godson of a high-ranking officer can be recruited as an undercover agent. With access to confidential data on security operations and strategies, he could obtain resources of interest to the intelligence agency and pass them discreetly, taking advantage of his family or other relationship with his protector.

As you may have discovered, spies or secret agents, camouflaged or disguised as usual jobs, are among us more than we imagine, but their function is important and necessary for the protection and security of the community. They know that their work will rarely be publicly recognized, but this does not diminish their enthusiasm or commitment to their work. They act motivated by the collective well-being, and every interaction and observation they make is essential to preserve the sovereignty and security of the nation.

Analysis of data

When you sign in to your Netflix account, you receive content suggestions that are highly relevant and engaging to you, based on your specific interests. This simplifies the task of discovering new titles that may interest you, improving your online entertainment experience and strengthening your loyalty to the platform.

Data analytics is a critical tool that companies like Netflix use to provide you with personalized movie and TV show recommendations. By tracking your viewing history, genre preferences, ratings, and demographics, Netflix generates suggestions tailored to your individual tastes.

This example illustrates how data analytics is not limited to intelligence operations, but is also applied in industries such as entertainment, where it contributes to customer satisfaction and service quality.

In the intelligence realm, once information is collected, agencies employ expert analysts to examine and evaluate this data with the goal of transforming raw information into actionable intelligence. This involves identifying relevant patterns, trends and relationships in the data to better understand threats and opportunities. In addition, it allows you to evaluate the credibility of information, prioritize resources and take proactive measures to mitigate risks and take advantage of opportunities. In short, its purpose is to convert data into meaningful knowledge that guides effective and efficient actions.

In an increasingly digitalized world, electronic communications play an important role in intelligence gathering. From **emails** to **phone calls** to **text messages,** every bit can contain valuable clues about potential threats, criminal activities or geopolitical movements, each electronic interaction leaves a trail that can be collected and analyzed by intelligence agencies.

Although it may sound like something out of a spy movie, electronic communications monitoring, which we will discuss in more detail elsewhere in this book, is an everyday reality in the fight against organized crime, terrorism, and other threats to protect the national security and the well-being of society.

Data analysis in intelligence is essential to understanding and making informed decisions in the field of security, strategy and government decision-making. Here I explain its main utilities:

- **Identify patterns and trends:** Helps you see how people behave, how they are connected, and what new things are happening in large groups of data. These patterns may be indicative of suspicious activities or potential threats.

- **Predict future threats:** By analyzing historical and real-time data, intelligence agencies can foresee possible future threats and events, allowing them to take preventive measures to protect the population.
- **Intelligence gathering:** Facilitates the collection and organization of information from various sources, such as intercepted communications, financial records, social networks, and more. This provides a more complete understanding of the environments and activities of interest.
- **Decision support:** Provides critical information and analysis that supports strategic and operational decision-making regarding national security and defense. It is also very useful in the business world.
- **Cyber threat Identification:** Helps identify and mitigate cyber challenges by analyzing data related to malicious activities, security vulnerabilities, and anomalous behavior in networks and computer systems.

Like a puzzle that is assembled from scattered pieces to form a complete picture, data analytics is essential for security, stability, and decision-making. In the world of intelligence agencies, data is the basis on which strategic decisions are made, threats are assessed, and society is protected.

Data quality is the foundation of this process. Imagine analysts as modern miners, extracting intellectual gold from raw data. Accurate, up-to-date and reliable data is vital for predicting trends, identifying patterns and anticipating risks. Without them, intelligence agencies would be sailing blindly in a sea of uncertainty.

Behind every classified report, security alert, and covert

operation, there is a team dedicated to ensuring data integrity. Data quality is more than a technical requirement; It is a matter of citizen protection and national security.

Intelligence generation

Amazon intensively uses data analysis to understand its customers' preferences and behaviors. Every time you browse their website or make purchases online, the platform tracks and records all your clicks, from the products you look at to the ones you add to cart and finally purchase.

With this information, Amazon can generate personalized recommendations for each user, showing related or suggested products that may be of interest to them. It uses advanced algorithms to forecast future purchases and adjust your inventory and marketing strategies accordingly.

Additionally, data analytics allows Amazon to optimize its supply chain and logistics, anticipating product demand and ensuring items are available when customers need them. Thus, the company improves the customer experience, increases sales and optimizes its operations in all areas of its business.

Both Amazon and intelligence agencies use data analysis to **better understand their users and customers** and to improve their operations. Both entities collect a large amount of data from various sources and analyze it to extract meaningful information that allows them to make informed decisions.

For example, Amazon analyzes its customers' purchasing behavior to anticipate their needs and offer personalized product recommendations. Similarly, intelligence agencies collect information from various sources, such as electronic signals, intercepted communications, and human sources, and analyze it to identify patterns, trends, and potential threats.

Additionally, both Amazon and intelligence agencies are investing in advanced technologies, such as machine learning and artificial intelligence, to improve their analysis capabilities and obtain more accurate and timely information. In summary, both entities share the ability to generate intelligence from data analysis, although with different purposes and application contexts. One does it to improve your shopping experience, and the others do it to protect and make informed decisions.

Social Networks and Open-Source Intelligence
Social media has changed the way we communicate and share information, but it has also opened up new opportunities for intelligence gathering. Law enforcement agencies can use data analysis algorithms to examine millions of posts, comments, and profiles for behavioral patterns, emerging trends, or signs of suspicious activity. Thus, that seemingly innocuous post you shared on your social media profile may be part of a set of data that intelligence services are analyzing for relevant information.

There are several examples of how social media has been used for intelligence gathering and monitoring electronic communications. Here are some cases:

- **The Arab Spring:** During the Arab Spring uprisings in several Middle Eastern and North African countries in 2010 and 2011, social media played a significant role in organizing and coordinating protests. Governments used social media monitoring to track protester activity and prevent potential unrest. Additionally, foreign intelligence services were also able to gather information on the protests and assess the political landscape in the region through analysis of social media data.
- **The Boston Bombing:** After the Boston Marathon bombing in 2013, social media data analysis was used to investigate the perpetrators and their connections. Intelligence agencies collected information from social networks such as Twitter, now X, and Facebook

to identify possible links to extremist groups and analyze patterns of behavior that could indicate suspicious activity.
- **Terrorist attacks in Europe:** In several terrorist attacks in Europe, such as those in Paris in 2015 and in Brussels in 2016, data analysis on social networks was used to track the activity of those responsible and their contacts. Authorities collected information from platforms such as Twitter, now X, Facebook and Instagram to identify potential conspirators, analyze their interactions and prevent future attacks.

These examples illustrate how social media has become an important source of intelligence for security agencies and how data analysis on these platforms can help in detecting behavioral patterns, emerging trends and suspicious activities.

Social media data analysis is an invaluable tool in open-source intelligence (OSINT), as it allows you to collect, analyze and understand relevant information efficiently and in real time. Here I present some key points about the usefulness of this type of analysis in open-source intelligence:

- **Information gathering:** Social networks are a rich source of data generated by users around the world. From posts on Twitter, now X, to status updates on Facebook, these platforms offer a wealth of information that can be useful in understanding trends, public opinions, current events, and more.
- **Identification of trends and patterns:** Data analysis on social networks allows us to identify emerging trends, behavioral patterns and changes in public opinion. By monitoring topical tags or *hashtags*, conversation topics, and interactions between users, analysts can detect important events or areas of interest that require attention.
- **Detection of threats and risks:** Monitoring

conversations on social networks can help identify possible threats or security risks. For example, intelligence agencies can detect the planning of violent events, the spread of disinformation, or the radicalization of individuals through their online activities.
- **Profiling of individuals and groups:** Social media data analysis allows for the creation of detailed profiles of individuals and groups, which can be useful for intelligence or law enforcement investigations. By examining a person or entity's online activities, analysts can gain insights into their interests, affiliations, connections, and behaviors.
- **Real-time event tracking:** Social media offers a real-time window into events happening around the world. Data analysis on these platforms allows intelligence agencies to monitor events such as protests, natural disasters or armed conflicts, facilitating decision-making and rapid response to emergency situations.

In summary, social media data analysis is a powerful tool in open-source intelligence, allowing intelligence agencies to collect information, identify trends, detect threats and risks, profile individuals and groups, and track events in real time to maintain the safety and well-being of society.

The social networks most commonly used for data analysis in open-source intelligence vary by region and specific context, but some of the most popular platforms include:

- **Twitter, now called X:** has become a primary source of data for intelligence analysis, thanks to its instant publishing capacity and the diversity of topics it covers. With around **330 million** active users per month and more than **500 million** tweets sent daily, Twitter offers an immense wealth of information. Hashtags and **mentions** on Twitter, now under the name X, are exceptional tools for monitoring conversations about current events, developing trends, and the pulse of public opinion.

- **Facebook:** Although some information on Facebook is protected behind privacy settings, this social network remains a rich source of publicly accessible data. With more than **2.8 billion** active users each month, the platform is a hive of everyday interactions. Public groups, news pages and events are open windows to understanding the activities, interests and perspectives of participants.

- **YouTube:** This multimedia content giant is vital for its diversity of materials, including news videos, public speeches and documentaries. With an audience of more than **two billion** monthly active members and more than **one billion** hours of videos watched each day, YouTube is a treasure trove of data. The study of comments, number of views and metadata of the videos can reveal valuable trends about the interests and predominant opinions at a given moment.

- **Instagram:** A popular photo and video sharing platform, which offers unique perspectives on events, destinations and participants' activities. With a community of more than **one billion** active users per month and more than **500 million** stories published every day, the analysis of *hashtags*, geolocations and mentions is key to deciphering digital trends and behaviors.

- **TikTok:** This dynamic social media platform makes it easy to create and spread short videos. With an audience exceeding one billion monthly active creators, it has captured the attention of the young generation, becoming an epicenter for viral video trends, entertainment, music and pop culture. For intelligence analysis, it is a gold mine due to its highly shared content and rapidly changing trends.

- **LinkedIn:** This social network is the hub of the professional world, where users exchange information about their careers, establish work connections, and stay up to date with industry news. With more than **800 million** professionals in more than **200 countries** and territories, LinkedIn is an invaluable resource for intelligence analysis. Close examination of profiles, networks, and updates can provide crucial insights into understanding trends and movements in the workplace and corporate environment.

- **Reddit:** A content embedding platform where members can submit, vote, and comment on links and posts. With more than **430 million** monthly active users, Reddit is notable for its specialized topic communities, known as *subreddits*, that address a wide variety of interests and topics. Analyzing discussions, votes, and comments on Reddit can be extremely useful in understanding public opinions, identifying emerging trends, and monitoring current events in various areas of interest.

These are just some of the most used social networks for data analysis in open-source intelligence. Depending on the context and objectives of the investigation, intelligence agencies can use a variety of platforms to gather relevant information and gain a more complete understanding of current events and trends.

With this exponential growth in online presence, the ability to monitor, analyze and participate in real-time conversations has become crucial to maintaining a competitive advantage and a meaningful connection with target audiences. Then the need arises to apply specialized tools to optimize performance in data analysis on social networks.

If you work for a government institution or a company that has a marketing and advertising department or are involved with any market research or analysis entity, pay close attention, because the technological solutions that I share with you below, and that will never tell you an intelligence agency, they will save you a lot of time and money.

Next, I'll show you some of the main tools available for social media management and analysis, such as Hootsuite, Buffer, Brandwatch, Sprout Social, Talkwalker, Meltwater and Crimson Hexagon (Brandwatch Consumer Research), highlighting its main characteristics and its usefulness in the current landscape of social networks. With these platforms, in addition to scheduling your posts and performing data analysis, you can take advantage of their advanced functionalities for tracking mentions, identifying emerging trends, sentiment analysis, and identifying influencers, providing you with a comprehensive and detailed view of the behavior of your users. your target audience online.

Let's look at its particularities in more detail:

- **Hootsuite**: It is a comprehensive solution that allows you to monitor multiple social networks, schedule posts, perform data analysis, and manage user engagement from a single interface. It is especially useful for real-time monitoring of conversations on networks such as Twitter, now X, Facebook, Instagram and LinkedIn. Its advanced features include mention tracking, trend identification, audience sentiment measurement, and detailed performance analysis of published content.
- **Buffer**: Similar to Hootsuite, Buffer allows you to schedule posts across multiple social networks and

provides performance analytics to evaluate the impact of posts. It is extremely useful for monitoring social media activity. Its intuitive interface and ability to identify optimal publishing times help you optimize reach and audience engagement and save resources.

- **Brandwatch**: Recognized for its advanced social media analytics capabilities, Brandwatch offers mention tracking, sentiment analysis, influencer identification, and emerging trend detection. It is especially useful for understanding public perception on specific topics and conducting competitive analysis and adjusting your strategies accordingly.

- **Sprout Social**: Provides a robust set of tools for social media management, data analysis, and custom reporting. It allows you to monitor the activity of multiple social accounts, measure the impact of campaign performance and identify opportunities for interaction and engagement of the target audience.

- **Talkwalker**: Uses advanced algorithms to identify trends and patterns in large volumes of social data, provide real-time analytics, brand tracking, and influencer identification. Ideal for institutions and companies interested in managing their online reputation.

- **Meltwater**: Specializes in media monitoring and social media analysis to help companies and organizations understand public opinion, identify potential crises, and measure the impact of marketing campaigns. Its advanced tools provide a detailed view of the digital landscape.

- **Crimson Hexagon (Brandwatch Consumer Research)**: Provides in-depth social media analysis, including audience segmentation and detection of emerging topics. It is useful to understand the attitudes and behaviors of the target audience.

These are just a few of the many tools available, as social media is a rich source of data and insights, and there are a variety of platforms designed to extract and analyze this crucial information. The choice of the optimal solution depends on the requirements of the intelligence analyst and the strategic objectives of the investigation. Therefore, I recommend that you explore different alternatives and try various options until you find the one that aligns with your needs.

For governments and intelligence agencies, the selection of social media analytics platforms can be influenced by factors such as operational needs, procurement policies, and available budgets. Despite the diversity of options, some tools and platforms have gained popularity among governments for their effectiveness and accuracy, including:

- **Palantir:** Although it is not designed exclusively for social media management, its application in the government sector is extensive. It allows you to integrate, visualize and analyze large volumes of information from a variety of sources. This capability includes the ability to ingest and examine social media data, making it a valuable tool for understanding complex social dynamics and global trends.

- **Dataminr:** Specializes in providing real-time alerts, essential for making critical decisions. By analyzing data from social networks and integrating with other sources of public information, this platform is a strategic ally for government agencies. Its cutting-edge event detection technology allows us to identify emerging trends and react promptly to situations that could affect national security. Its ability to filter and analyze large amounts of data in real time makes it an indispensable tool in the field of intelligence and risk prevention.

- **NC4**: Excels in the area of situational intelligence and threat analysis, providing organizations with the ability to monitor critical events in real time and evaluate potential risks effectively. This platform is particularly valuable for governments and corporate entities, offering security intelligence solutions tailored to their needs. It includes detailed analysis of social networks, allowing early detection of threats and implementation of preventive measures. NC4's ability to provide a comprehensive view of risks and when they are occurring makes it an essential tool for proactive security management.

- **Media Sonar**: Offers an exhaustive analysis of social networks and the dark web, key tools for identifying potential threats. Facilitates high-level intelligence investigations and strengthens cybersecurity operations. Its ability to analyze data from multiple digital sources allows you to proactively detect threats and monitor suspicious online activities. As a result, it provides valuable and applicable information that is essential for public safety and security.

- **Sysomos**: It is widely recognized in the field of marketing for its customer analysis capabilities. However, its usefulness transcends this area, since government agencies also use it for its advanced social network analysis functionalities. The platform is effective in monitoring and examining conversations on matters of public relevance. Its tools allow you to follow trends, measure general sentiment and detect influential figures, which is interesting, especially when political and military leaders are interested in understanding and managing social dynamics in various contexts.

It is essential to recognize that the use of social network analysis tools by government entities is regulated by privacy policies and specific legislation. Accessing and using social media data for intelligence purposes must be done with a keen ethical awareness, as significant concerns around privacy and individual rights may arise. Therefore, it is imperative that governments exercise due diligence and transparency when implementing these technologies, ensuring that their use is aligned with ethical principles and current regulations.

Intelligence and Social Engineering Agencies
Social engineering and manipulation of will are increasingly present phenomena in our digital society. These terms refer to the psychological manipulation of individuals or groups to obtain confidential information, induce certain behaviors, or persuade them to perform specific actions.

In an environment where our personal information is readily available online, social media data has become a powerful tool for those practicing social engineering. Here are some ways you can be a victim of social engineering:

- **Extraction of sensitive information:** Through deception, attackers could try to persuade you to reveal sensitive data, such as passwords or personal information, which can be exploited in fraud or cybercrime.

- **Manipulation of perceptions and behaviors:** Through social engineering, erroneous or misleading information can be spread on social networks, seeking to alter the opinions and behaviors of people like you and me. This includes the spread of fake news and the manipulation of public discussions.

- **Identity forgery:** Cybercriminals often pose as

legitimate individuals or entities on social media, in order to trick you into gaining access to inside information or conduct fraudulent activities on their behalf.

- **Network and system penetration:** It can also be used to infiltrate computer networks and systems by deceiving employees or other authorized users, which may involve sending phishing emails *or* creating fake websites designed to confuse you and you fall into their trap.

To protect citizens against such threats, intelligence agencies play a vital role. Using advanced data analysis techniques, patterns of suspicious online behavior are detected that could indicate attempts at manipulation or social engineering. By monitoring social media and other online platforms, unusual or anomalous activities are identified that could pose a threat to the safety of individuals or society as a whole.

These agencies also play an important role in educating and raising awareness about these dangers, offering resources and advice to strengthen cybersecurity and minimize vulnerability to these types of attacks.

It is essential to implement key measures to identify and protect citizens who could be victims of social engineering, such as:

- **Education and awareness:** Inform citizens about social engineering tactics and how to recognize them, identifying red flags and promoting safe online practices.
- **Staff training:** Train staff to identify and respond to potential threats, through *phishing drills* and other training activities.
- **Suspicious activity monitoring:** Detect unusual online activities, using data analysis tools to identify

patterns of suspicious behavior in cyberspace.

- **Intersectoral collaboration:** Alliances with the private sector to exchange information on threats and develop strategies with technology companies on the subject.

- **Development of protection tools:** Innovate in security technologies, creating advanced tools and technologies to help citizens protect themselves against social engineering, such as multi-factor authentication systems and more sophisticated antivirus *software*.

It is also recommended that users be aware of these tactics and take concrete steps to protect themselves against social engineering. Below, I share some simple actions you can take:

- **Review privacy settings:** Be sure to review and adjust the privacy settings on your social media accounts to limit the amount of personal information you share publicly.

- **Online security education:** Research and take advantage of the resources available online against cybercrime. Actively participate in educational programs that delve into effective methods to counter social engineering and other digital dangers.

- **Updated Information:** Get up to date on the latest tactics and trends in social engineering so you can recognize and avoid potential online attacks.

- **Report suspicious activities:** If you notice suspicious activities online, such as requests for personal information or strange behavior on social media, be sure to report it to authorities or online platforms as soon as possible.

By strengthening awareness and defenses against these measures, the risk of citizens being manipulated or deceived online can be reduced, thus protecting the will and security of society in an increasingly complex and connected digital environment. Together we can do the difference!

Books / movies and series - 60 key facts

[The pillars of intelligence]

BOOKS:

1. **"Tinker Tailor Soldier Spy"** - John le Carré, 2014

This very famous spy novel that takes place in the 70s, during the Cold War, of moles and lamplighters, scalp hunters and street artists, where men are changed, burned and bought. It focuses on the search for a spy infiltrated at the top of MI6.

After the failure of a special mission in Hungary, there is a change at the top of the British secret services. The protagonist is George Smiley, a retired veteran agent of the British Secret Intelligence Service, also known as MI6 or SIS who, despite having been separated, is required for a special mission: Find out who the "mole" infiltrated the dome is. from service.

With the help of other retired agents, Smiley gathers information and puts together the pieces necessary to discover the traitor. The story is a complex game of espionage and intrigue that reflects the tension and mistrust of the Cold War. The novel has been adapted into a television series and a film, and is a benchmark in the espionage genre. Available on Amazon https://amzn.to/3IYWLoo

2. **"The Craft of Intelligence"** - Allen W. Dulles, 1963

This work written by Allen W. Dulles, who was director of the United States Central Intelligence Agency (CIA) between 1953 and 1961, is a classic of its genre, considered by many to be one of the most didactic and fascinating books of all. time.

Addresses the evolution of intelligence and espionage in the United States, offering an inside view of CIA operations and strategies during the Cold War. While exposing how the United States, despite having only 6% of the world's population, owned 50% of the world's wealth at the time.

Explains the task of collection, how information is obtained and how it is processed. Analyzes the intelligence agencies of the Soviet Union and other communist countries, counterespionage, the art of spying during the Cold War, and the necessary balance between national security and individual freedom in a free society. Available on Amazon https://amzn.to/3J2st4h

3. **"Secrets of Navajo Code Talkers"** - Rachael L. Thomas, 2023

This interesting book, "Secrets of the Navajo Code Talkers", offers a unique insight into how intelligence agencies, particularly the United States Navy, used the Navajo language as an encryption tool during World War II. The Navajo Marines created a code based on their native language, an indigenous North American language that exists to this day, which proved to be an advanced, radio-indecipherable mechanism for the Japanese enemy.

In times of war, unbreakable codes help armies win battles. The book details how these Marines risked their lives to translate secret messages during the war. It also explains why the Navajo language was ideal for encoding messages, with a sample of the special vocabulary that coders used in battle.

The film "War Codes" or *Windtalkers,* starring Nicolas Cage, based on real events, serves to understand how orders were transmitted to Navajo translators, and they issued them in their language to other Navajo operators from other divisions (artillery, aviation, command base, battalions etc.) on Saipan during World War II, so that the Japanese never managed to decipher. The book is available on Amazon https://amzn.to/4cC8Ayw

4. **"Spy Women: Intrigues and Sabotage Behind Enemy**

Lines"* - Laura Manzanera, 2008

The publication "Women Spies: Intrigues and Sabotage Behind Enemy Lines" challenges the stereotypical image of female spies as simple seductresses, presenting a fascinating account of how women have played essential roles in the secret services since ancient times.

Throughout its 448 pages, the book addresses the topic of intelligence agencies, highlighting the stories of women from different eras and nationalities, who, motivated by patriotism, idealism, a desire for adventure, love or revenge, have been the protagonists of episodes crucial to history.

The author collects emblematic examples such as Virginia de Castiglione, who lay on the bed of Napoleon III for the independence of Italy; or Belle Boyd, who walked through the crossfire to deliver a message to General Jackson; or Josephine Baker, who traveled throughout Europe with hidden messages in the scores of her show.

Spy Women is a meritorious recognition of the role of the left hand, as well as an interesting tour of the adventures of the best spies in history. Available on Amazon with this link: https://amzn.to/3TXSEPG

5. *"InvestiGators: Agents of S.U.I.T."* - John Patrick Green, 2020

The book "InvestiGators: Agents of SUIT" is an expansion of the universe of the "InvestiGators" graphic novel series, aimed at young readers, which presents the adventures of Mango and Brash, two crocodile detectives who are part of a secret agency called S.U.I.T. (Special Undercover Investigation Teams). Your mission is to solve mysteries and protect the city from villains who try to cause trouble. It is originally written in English, with more than 10 publications.

The book addresses the topic of intelligence agencies through the adventures of these characters, highlighting how field agents play a crucial role in solving mysteries and protecting society.

So far, the following 4 titles have been translated into Spanish: "*InvestiGators 1 - Agentes con muchos dientes*", "*InvestiGators 2 - De cabeza al váter*", "*InvestiGators 3 - Hasta luego, cocodrilo*" y "*InvestiGators 4 - Hormigas contra robots*". The complete series is available on Amazon in English https://amzn.to/3xpl8Ji and in Spanish here: https://amzn.to/3TVujtQ

FILMS:

1. ***"Tinker Tailor Soldier Spy"*** – (United Kingdom, 2012)
[Research and analysis]

"Tinker Tailor Soldier Spy", also known as "The Spy Who Knew Too Much" or "The Mole", is a suspense drama set in the 1970s, during the Cold War, after a special mission in Hungary fails and causes changes in the British secret services. Retired agent George Smiley is recruited to discover the identity of a "mole" infiltrated at the top of the Service. The film addresses topics such as surveillance, ethical dilemmas and personal change in a context of political oppression, highlighting the importance of intelligence analysis and the ability to discern between truth and lies. Starring Gary Oldman, Mark Strong and John Hurt, this film offers a fascinating exploration of the complicated aspects of espionage during this crucial period in world history. You can watch it on HBO Max and Apple TV. Depending on your location, you could get it for free on other platforms like YouTube or Vudu.

2. **"SEAL Team Six"** - Geronimo Code: The Hunt for Bin Laden (USA, 2012)
[Interagency coordination]

"SEAL Team Six" Chronicle of the Hunt for Osama Bin Laden, known by the code name "Operation Geronimo" is a television film that chronicles the covert mission carried out by the United States SEAL Team to capture or eliminate the leader of Al-Qaeda and responsible for the attacks of September 11, 2001. The plot focuses on the preparations, planning and execution of the military operation that culminated in the death of Bin Laden in 2011. The film offers a dramatized representation of the events, based in publicly available information and in testimonies of people involved in the operation. It stars William Fichtner, Cam Gigandet, Kenneth Miller and others, highlighting the importance of interagency coordination on high-risk missions like this. You can get it on Amazon Prime Video and Apple TV.

3. *"True Lies"* – (USA, 1994)

[Undercover agent]

"True Lies" is a thrilling action-comedy thriller that follows the life of a government special agent with a double identity. While leading a seemingly ordinary life as an insurance salesman, he is actually a skilled international spy working for Omega, a top-secret agency tasked with countering nuclear terrorism. Played by Arnold Schwarzenegger, the protagonist is faced with the difficult task of keeping his secret life away from his family, especially his wife, played by Jamie Lee Curtis. When their two worlds collide, a series of events is unleashed that drags them both into a dangerous terrorist plot, putting everything they love at risk. You can find it on various streaming service platforms such as Netflix, Amazon Prime Video, HBO, Disney+ YouTube and others.

4. *"Ghosting"* - Ghosted (USA, 2023)

[Woman in Special Operations]

"Ghosting" is an action romantic comedy that follows Ana de Armas in the role of a cunning CIA agent, in a female version reminiscent of 007. Alongside her is Chris Evans, the former Captain America, playing a man charming man who falls deeply in love with this enigmatic secret agent. Before they can go on a second date, they become involved in an exciting international adventure to save the world. The film offers exciting action scenes inspired by productions like John Wick, as the couple fights against time and enemies to complete their mission and find more than just romance in the process. It is original Apple TV content.

5. *"My Spy"* – (USA, 2020)

[Surveillance operation]

In the action comedy "My Spy", a demoted CIA agent is forced to keep an eye on a 9-year-old girl. However, when the girl discovers his true identity, instead of exposing him, she blackmails him into training her and teaching her to be cooler in school. Although the film does not pretend to be realistic, it offers a fun insight into the world of espionage and highlights the importance of technology in this field. Starring Dave Bautista and Chloe Coleman in the lead roles, the film promises moments of action and laughter as the unlikely couple embark on unexpected adventures. Available on Amazon Prime Video.

SERIES:

1. *"Patriot"* – (USA, 2017)

[18 Episodes | 2 Seasons]

"Patriot" stands out for its unique approach of mixing dark humor with moments of intense drama. The story focuses on the Tavner family, with special attention to John Tavner, an Iraq War veteran who works as an undercover intelligence officer. Its mission is to prevent Iran from developing nuclear weapons. To achieve this, John infiltrates a Luxembourg-based industrial company, posing as a pipeline analyst. However, as the mission progresses, personal and professional complications arise that endanger both its goal and its own sanity.

The series offers a fresh and original take on the spy genre, with complex characters and an intriguing narrative. From the perspective of John Tavner, it explores topics such as post-traumatic stress, morality in intelligence work, and the complexities of family relationships. It combines elements of comedy, espionage and suspense, providing a unique perspective on the challenges and tensions that intelligence agents face in their work. You can watch "Patriot" on Amazon Prime Video. I also recommend checking JustWatch to see if it is available on other platforms like Filmin or Apple TV.

2. **"Burn Notice"** - Latest Notice | Stuck in Miami | Operation Miami (USA, 2007)

[111 Episodes | 7 Seasons]

Although "Burn Notice" did not win any big-name awards, had a loyal fan base throughout its 7 seasons, and was appreciated for its mix of humor, espionage, and drama. The plot follows Michael Westen, a former spy who is suddenly "burned" or fired and uses his special abilities to help others in trouble. This way, you can cover the costs of your personal research in parallel.

With no idea why or who has decided to withdraw him, with no past or money, and unable to use his usual contacts and forced not to leave the city,

He is determined to find out the reason for his sudden dismissal and, perhaps, find a way to rejoin the agency he belonged to. If you are one of those lovers of action and wit, "Burn Notice" offers a thrilling look into the life of a former undercover agent. The complete series in Spanish is available on Disney Plus.

3. **"Homeland"** – (USA, 2011)

[96 Episodes | 8 Seasons]

"Homeland", considered one of the best dramas of recent years, has been awarded five Golden Globe Awards and eight Emmy Awards. The series is inspired by the acclaimed Israeli series "Hatufim". It centers on Marine Sergeant Nicholas Brody, who returns home eight years after he went missing in Iraq. His return raises questions about whether he has gone over to the enemy and now represents a risk to national security.

In "Homeland", you will follow Carrie Mathison, a CIA officer, in her fight against terrorism and complex international conspiracies, where electronic monitoring is essential to prevent catastrophes. The series explores themes such as espionage, terrorism, morality and the complexities of family relationships. You can watch "Homeland" on Disney Plus or check out other platforms like JustWatch or Filmaffinity to find additional options.

4. **"Hatufim"** - Prisoners of War (ISR, 2011)

[24 Episodes | 2 Seasons]

The Israeli television series "Hatufim", known in English as "Prisoners of War", inspired the American television drama "Homeland". The plot focuses on the story of three Israeli soldiers who were captured during a mission in Lebanon and held as prisoners of war for 17 years. After they are released and repatriated to Israel, the series follows their lives, focusing on their difficult process of reintegration into society and their families. It explores the lasting emotional and psychological effects of captivity, as well as the secrets and traumas both soldiers and their families face as they try to rebuild their lives. Additionally, it examines the ethical dilemmas and emotional complexities surrounding prisoners of war and their loved ones, while exploring themes such as loyalty, identity, forgiveness and redemption.

"Hatufim" received critical acclaim for its calm, slow, and realistic style, as well as its focus on soldiers and families affected by war. It is considered one of the most influential productions on Israeli television. You can enjoy it on Hulu, Apple TV and Netflix in Israel.

5. **"Danger Mouse"** – (UK, 1981)

[161 Episodes | 10 Seasons]

"Danger Mouse" is a British animated series that follows the adventures of the world's most secret English secret agent, the brave and bold Danger Mouse, and his shy, but loyal sidekick, Penfold. Together, they work to protect the world from all manner of villains and threats, using a combination of ingenuity, spy skills, and futuristic gadgets. It is packed with humor and action, with comical situations and exciting missions that keep viewers entertained. "Danger Mouse" is a classic series that has been loved by generations of children and remains popular today.

The original series aired from 1981 to 1992, but there was also a reboot in 2015 that continued the story with new adventures. Episodes of "Danger Mouse" can be found on Netflix, Amazon Prime Video, Apple TV, Google TV and YouTube. It may also be available on on-demand TV streaming services, depending on your location.

In this chapter, we have explored the pillars that underpin the complex process of intelligence agency operations around the world. These organizations, whose work transcends the conventional limits of the State, are based on three essential pillars: information collection, data analysis and intelligence generation.

Gathering information is the crucial first step in the process. It ranges from open-sources accessible to the public to classified sources with restricted access, providing agencies with a complete and accurate view of the situation at hand. This process of actively and passively searching for data is essential to efficiently address national security challenges.

Once the information is collected, the experts enter the data analysis phase. Here, they thoroughly examine the collected data to identify patterns, trends, and potential threats. This process, which requires strong analytical skills and the use of advanced tools such as predictive analytics software and artificial intelligence systems, is critical to extracting meaningful insights from the deluge of available material.

Finally, we come to intelligence generation, where analysts transform operational data and resources into relevant and critical information for decision makers. This intelligence is transcendental in the formulation of policies and strategies, contributing directly to national security and the well-being of society.

The role of intelligence agencies is fundamental in our daily lives, although it often goes unnoticed. From crime prevention to international crisis anticipation, these organizations work tirelessly to provide critical information that helps protect the nation's security and well-being. Their work, based on a combination of surveillance, analysis and intelligence generation, has a direct impact on our security and quality of life.

To deepen your understanding of the fascinating world of intelligence agencies, I invite you to explore some of the suggested films or series. Additionally, I would love for you to share your reflections and comments in the book review forum on Amazon. Your opinion is valuable and may help other readers make an informed decision about this book.

In the next chapter, we will continue to explore fundamental issues related to global security and the challenges facing intelligence agencies in the contemporary world. You will learn about cyber intelligence, counterespionage, counterterrorism and much more. Are you ready to dive into the world of digital espionage and cybersecurity?

CHAPTER 3: INTELLIGENCE OPERATIONS AND GLOBAL SECURITY

Like invisible pillars that support the roof of global security under which we all shelter, the influence of these entities extends from the highest levels of government to the streets we walk every day.

Its agents work boldly to anticipate and neutralize threats that could disrupt our daily routines, from terrorist attacks to human-induced natural disasters. By doing so, they allow society to focus on development and well-being without constant concern for its safety.

The peace of mind with which we travel, the confidence in economic stability, and the protection of our online privacy are just some of the ways in which intelligence agencies influence our lives.

In this chapter, I will reveal some secrets about the impact these activities have on stability and security at the local, national and global levels. With historical and current case examples, we will illustrate its indispensable role in key geopolitical events. Although their work is discreet, these entities are silent architects of the course of history and fundamental pillars for harmony and security in our increasingly interconnected world.

We will delve into how covert operations, intelligence gathering, and collaboration with foreign intelligence agencies influence foreign policy and international relations. Additionally, we will address the repercussions of cybersecurity and cyber espionage in the digital age, highlighting how intelligence agencies are adapting their strategies to confront emerging threats in this area.

Strategic Operations
If you were the owner of a small local food business and you notice that a nearby competitor is attracting more customers, despite offering a similar menu to yours. You suspect they might be using unfair tactics to gain an unfair advantage in the market.

You decide to carry out an **intelligence operation** to investigate this situation. You start by observing your competitor's business for several days to detect patterns of behavior and activity. You notice that a large number of people enter and leave the establishment in a short period of time, but you cannot identify any unique characteristic that explains its success.

Next, you decide to talk to some customers who frequent both businesses to get information about their experience. You discover that some customers have received special offers and exclusive discounts when visiting your competitor's business, which could explain why they are attracting more customers.

With this information, you proceed to adjust your *marketing strategy* and offer similar promotions to attract more customers to your business. You also consider reporting your competitor's unfair business practices to the relevant authorities, if necessary.

Just as a restaurant owner watches his competitors, studies market trends, and talks to his customers to improve his business, government intelligence agencies gather information from various sources to understand the threats, opportunities, and challenges facing the country.

Both must be attentive to changes in the environment, detect hidden patterns and anticipate possible risks to remain competitive and safe. Whether it is detecting unfair tactics in the market or preventing terrorist activities, intelligence is essential for effective decision making and protecting the interests of both the business and the country.

This analogy helps illustrate how intelligence operations, although often associated with government and national security, also have parallels in people's daily lives, demonstrating their relevance and applicability in various contexts.

Strategic operations of intelligence agencies are planned and executed actions to protect national security, prevent threats and promote the country's interests in the international arena. These covert operations cover various areas, such as **counterespionage**, **counterterrorism**, **cyber intelligence** and the collection of strategic information.

It is crucial that citizens understand the strategic operations of intelligence agencies, as they provide a window into methods of protecting their security and well-being at all levels. Knowing how these activities work fosters awareness about current threats, how they are faced and the measures implemented to defend the population.

Understanding counterespionage is contributing to the safeguarding of national secrets and sensitive information from foreign espionage. Becoming familiar with counterterrorism operations provides peace of mind, knowing that there are proactive efforts to prevent attacks and protect society. Furthermore, understanding cyber intelligence is empowering people to better defend themselves against digital threats and protect their personal information.

I am convinced that knowledge about the strategic operations of intelligence agencies provides citizens with a deeper understanding of risk management and the protection of national security, thus promoting a culture of security and a more resilient society.

Below, I will delve into how **counterespionage**, **counterterrorism**, and **cyber intelligence** directly impact the security and well-being of society at large, even in everyday situations that might go unnoticed.

Counterespionage focuses on detecting and neutralizing the espionage activities of other nations or entities that may compromise national security. This is similar to the protection of personal privacy and information security in the digital world, which is why it is necessary to take measures to prevent unauthorized access to sensitive data.

Counterterrorism involves the identification, prevention, deterrence and response to terrorist activities, protecting citizens from possible threats or attacks. Here it is more related to security at public events, the protection of critical infrastructures and emergency response, where intelligence is essential to anticipate and neutralize any attempted attack or sabotage.

Cyber intelligence focuses on collecting relevant information from online sources to understand and counter cyber threats. This involves protecting yourself against identity theft, online fraud and cyber attacks, where it is essential to be aware of the tactics and techniques used by cyber criminals.

With these simple examples I wanted to illustrate how the strategic operations of intelligence agencies have a direct impact on daily life by guaranteeing security and protection against various threats, both physical and virtual. Now let's move on to the next level!

Covert operations, essential elements in any intelligence agency's arsenal, are intertwined with people's daily lives in ways that often go unnoticed. In the pages that follow, you can explore how these operations are not only crucial to national security, but also reflect actions we take every day.

In personal life, these are similar to the measures we take to protect our private information. Just as agencies use aliases and disguises to hide their identity, we use usernames and passwords to protect our digital identity. The caution we exercise in sharing personal information online echoes the secrecy and concealment techniques of intelligence agents.

On a professional level, these tactics are reflected in the way companies protect their data and business strategies. Just as agents work in the shadows to obtain valuable information, professionals employ security and confidentiality protocols to preserve corporate secrets.

In the community, they are manifested in anonymous actions that contribute to collective well-being. Similar to how these entities act without public recognition to ensure safety, people participate in community initiatives, often without seeking credit, to help others and improve their environment.

These analogies demonstrate that covert operations and intelligence agencies have direct relevance to our daily lives. They teach us that, although not always visible, discreet actions and the protection of information are fundamental to security and well-being at all levels of society.

Counterintelligence

We have mentioned that one of the fundamental tasks of these organizations is counterespionage, also known as counterintelligence, aimed at identifying and neutralizing both internal and external threats against national security. This involves, among other things, detecting potential spies and preventing leaks of confidential information. Have you ever wondered how this is done in practice? Let me illustrate it for you with the following example:

Let's say you're participating in a team game where you compete against other groups in a series of physical and intellectual challenges. During one of the tests, you notice that a rival team always seems to be one step ahead, even in challenges that require strategy and planning.

You decide to apply counterespionage techniques to discover how they are gaining this advantage. You observe their movements and behaviors during challenges and notice that they always retreat to a secluded corner to discuss among themselves before each test. You also notice that they seem to receive messages on their cell phones just before starting each challenge.

You decide to approach some members of that team under the pretext of making friends and participating in their conversations. Through your interactions, you discover that they are receiving outside help from a coach who provides them with strategies and advice to overcome challenges.

With this information in hand, you inform the game organizers about the situation and provide them with evidence, such as screenshots of messages received by the rival team. The organizers investigate the matter and discover that the team was indeed receiving outside help, which is against the rules of the game.

As a result, the rival team is disqualified and measures are taken to prevent them from receiving outside help in the future. Thanks to your counterespionage application, fairness in the game is guaranteed and the integrity of the competition is protected.

We do that more often than we can imagine!

Let's say you are the manager of a very successful technology company that develops innovative products. And you'll find out that a competing company is trying to hire some of your most talented employees to steal your ideas and trade secrets. You wouldn't sit idly by. Let's be honest!

The most common thing is that to avoid this, you hire a team of security experts who monitor the communications and activities of employees, on the technological equipment that you have provided for them, to detect any signs that they are sharing confidential information with the competition.

You would also implement additional security measures, such as protecting important files with strong passwords and restricting access to only authorized employees. In this case, your company would be carrying out counterespionage operations to protect its assets and maintain its competitive advantage in the market.

I will conclude with my favorite example, which I often use in my classes on counterintelligence. It surely reminds you of that friend of yours who has a solid relationship with his/her "lifelong love" and begins to notice strange behaviors in his/her partner, such as moving away to answer some calls or guarding his/her phone more carefully than usual. These signs raise concerns in him/her, suggesting that he/she could be hiding something important from him/her.

When your friend's anxiety overcomes his/her values and moral principles, he/she gives in to temptation and makes the mistake of violating his/her partner's privacy and intimacy, discreetly checking his/her phone for suspicious messages or clues on social networks. Or worse yet, he/she has the "great idea" to break the law, becoming a secret detective to discover the truth. You install a monitoring application on your partner's phone to record messages and calls, or even GPS, cameras or other devices, illegally carrying out counterespionage operations to investigate your partner's possible infidelity.

After a careful and stealthy investigation, using his/her counterespionage skills ingeniously, your friend discovers that his/her partner is planning a charming romantic surprise instead of a betrayal, thus confirming his/her suspicions that something abnormal was happening. But this experience leaves an important lesson: appearances can be deceiving!

I have always said that open and honest communication is essential to managing any concerns or mistrust in the relationship, so resorting to counterespionage without just cause can erode the couple's trust and bond. If you have legitimate concerns, it is advisable to address them directly and constructively through dialogue and open communication.

On the other hand, as a security specialist, I always recommend being alert to possible signs of mistrust or suspicious activities that may indicate that your partner is violating your privacy or trust. Here are some practical tips:

- **Communications review:** Be alert to changes in your partner's behavior around their electronic devices, such as excessive use of their phone or computer in private, frequently deleting their browsing history, or using passwords to protect their information.
- **Movement tracking:** Notice if your partner seems to be following your movements or trying to monitor your daily activities excessively, repeatedly asking where you are, checking your text messages or calls, checking your geolocation or Google Maps history, or showing up in unexpected places without a valid reason.
- **Collection of personal information:** Be aware of any attempts by your partner to collect personal information about you, search your belongings, check your email or messages, try to access your financial information, all of the above without your authorization.
- **Avoidant or defensive behavior:** Pay attention to

your partner's responses when asked about certain matters, especially if he or she avoids the topic, becomes defensive, or shows signs of nervousness when questioned.

It is essential to remember that trust and open communication are essential in any relationship. Resorting to counterespionage without a justified reason can weaken the couple's trust and bond, generating unnecessary tension and conflict.

We must be attentive to possible signs of mistrust or suspicious behavior in the couple, but without invading their privacy. Observing changes in behavior, movement tracking, personal information gathering, and avoidance behavior can help detect potential problems and address them before they become serious.

An honest and constructive tone of conversation is crucial, always maintaining mutual respect. Ultimately, maintaining a balance between surveillance and respect for each other's privacy is essential to maintaining a healthy and long-lasting relationship.

But do not limit it to your relationship, counterespionage techniques are applied in various ways in daily life to protect our privacy and family security and help you be alert to possible threats and preserve the confidentiality of sensitive information.

By watching for changes in your loved ones' behavior, such as excessive use of electronic devices, unauthorized surveillance of communications, or improper collection of personal information, you can detect potential suspicious activity that puts your safety at risk.

Furthermore, by fostering a culture of open communication at home, relationships are built based on trust and honesty, generating a more pleasant, safe and secure family environment.

Where to start? These steps, both digitally and physically, are a good start:

Digital scope:
- Use strong passwords and check the privacy settings on your online profiles to protect your personal information online.
- Keep security software on your electronic devices updated to prevent malware and remote spying.
- Avoid sharing sensitive data online and be cautious when interacting with strangers on social networks and online platforms.
- Use secure methods to store and transmit important content, such as end-to-end encryption and virtual private networks (VPN).
- Make regular backup copies of your data to the cloud or external devices to protect against loss or theft.

Physical environment:
- Keep an eye out for possible signs of surveillance in your surroundings, such as suspicious vehicles or people watching you repeatedly.
- Destroy sensitive documents before throwing them away and avoid sharing sensitive information with strangers to protect your privacy outside the digital realm.
- Perform electronic sweeps of your home or office to detect hidden listening devices.
- Watch for any unusual changes in your environment, such as out of place objects or flickering lights on your electronic devices, which could indicate unauthorized intrusions.
- Implement physical security measures, such as high-quality locks and alarm systems, to protect your home or office against intrusions and theft.

By applying these recommendations and maintaining an attitude of vigilance in your daily life and in your family environment, you improve your security and reduce the risk of being a victim of intrusions, fraud or privacy violations, both in your personal and digital environment.

Counterterrorism

A crucial operation carried out by intelligence agencies to protect critical infrastructure and ensure effective emergency response. Its main objective is to prevent and neutralize any attempted attack or sabotage. To achieve this, various strategies are used, ranging from infiltration of extremist organizations to exhaustive monitoring of suspicious communications.

Regarding the concept, there are debates among experts in the field. They propose that **counterterrorism** and **antiterrorism** are two complementary but different approaches in the fight against terrorism. Let's see their differences:

Counterterrorism: Focuses on preventing and deterring potential terrorist threats by gathering intelligence, infiltrating terrorist groups, and neutralizing plans before their execution. Seeks to prevent future attacks.

Counterterrorism: Focuses on responding to and mitigating the effects of terrorist acts that have already occurred. This includes the arrest of those responsible and the protection of the affected population. Its focus is to manage and counter the consequences of terrorist attacks already carried out.

Terrorism, in its constant evolution, has found new ways to manifest itself over time, especially with increasing access to technology. From its historical origins, marked by political movements and regional conflicts, to its transformation into a global threat with the influence of extremist ideologies and the rise of international terrorist groups, terrorism has constantly challenged the security and stability of societies around the world.

With the arrival of the digital age, terrorism has found the internet and social networks a platform to recruit, radicalize and coordinate attacks in a more efficient and global way. This change represents a significant challenge for intelligence agencies, which must constantly adapt to monitor and counter these new forms of terrorist threats. Their work becomes even more relevant in people's daily lives, as they work tirelessly to protect them from the invisible dangers that lurk in cyberspace and the physical world.

State intelligence services are essential in the detection and prevention of these acts, using meticulous analyzes to foresee and deactivate potential threats. Their work, although often invisible, is a constant safeguard for the safety of people, protecting their rights and freedoms and preserving social peace.

International collaboration between agencies reflects the interdependence inherent in our global society. It becomes a parallel to everyday interactions between individuals from different cultures and countries, demonstrating how cooperation transcends borders.

Just as people come together on social networks to share knowledge and experiences, or collaborate on projects that overcome geographic and cultural barriers, intelligence agencies form strategic alliances. These alliances are vital for sharing critical information and resources, strengthening collective capacity to confront global challenges.

In the professional field, international collaboration is manifested in multinational projects and in the synergy between companies from different nations, seeking to innovate and generate universal solutions. Intelligence agencies, collaborating with international entities, take a similar approach to combating borderless threats such as terrorism and cybercrime.

At the community level, international collaboration is evident in humanitarian aid and joint efforts to confront global challenges such as climate change. These institutions, working side by side with international partners, emphasize that joining forces is essential for global security and well-being.

In a world where terrorism knows no borders, the tireless vigilance of these personnel is more important than ever, forming a shield against the forces of fear and violence. Monitoring suspicious communications is crucial.

This proactive approach not only detects potential threats and prevents attacks, allows authorities to identify patterns of suspicious behavior, tracks the activity of extremist groups, but also deters potential terrorists by knowing they are being watched. This contributes to maintaining tranquility and stability in the communities, in addition to saving operational resources.

Cyber intelligence

It is the discipline that focuses on the collection, analysis and application of information related to threats and vulnerabilities in cyberspace.

Its main purpose is to identify, assess and mitigate potential risks and cyber attacks, all in order to safeguard digital assets and ensure online security.

This cyber intelligence process follows a scheme similar to that used in traditional intelligence operations in the physical sphere. Below, we break down the phases it includes:

- **Information gathering:** This stage covers a wide range of sources, from security event logs to *software vulnerability reports* and ethical hacking activities. Data collection is essential to obtain a complete view of the cyber landscape and potential threats.
- **Data analysis:** Once the data has been collected,

it is thoroughly analyzed. This analysis involves the identification of patterns, trends and possible cyber threats, as well as the evaluation of the credibility and relevance of the information. In addition, it seeks to identify possible adversary actors, attack methods and objectives.
- **Intelligence generation:** Based on data analysis, cyber intelligence is created that provides actionable information on threats and vulnerabilities. This intelligence can be manifested in risk reports, threat profiles and indicators of compromise, among others, and helps guide defense and protection strategies.
- **Intelligence application:** Cyber intelligence generated is used to inform cybersecurity decision making. This involves the development and implementation of defense strategies, as well as response to cyber incidents. Additionally, intelligence can be shared with other organizations to foster collaboration and coordination in the fight against cyber threats.

Cyber intelligence, with its proactive approach and its ability to anticipate and mitigate possible risks, is positioned as a vital tool in cyber protection in an increasingly interconnected and digitalized world.

But its usefulness is not limited to state agencies and large corporations. Below, I show you some practical examples of how cyber intelligence can be applied in people's daily lives:

- **Protection of personal data:** Using cyber intelligence techniques, such as email scanning, it is possible to verify the authenticity of the sender and analyze the links attached in suspicious emails before clicking, thus protecting you against possible phishing *or* malware attacks. For example, if you receive an email that seems suspicious, instead of clicking immediately, you decide to apply the techniques you learned, which allows you to detect and avoid a phishing attempt, thus safeguarding your data from possible cyber attacks.

Cyber intelligence is useful for monitoring the sensitive information you share on social networks. You can set alerts to detect unusual changes in privacy settings or activity on your profiles. If you notice someone accessing your information in an unauthorized manner or making changes to your privacy settings without your knowledge, you can take quick steps to protect your privacy and security online.

- **Prevention of industrial espionage:** In business or entrepreneurial environments, cyber intelligence plays a crucial role in facilitating the early detection of possible information leaks.

In protecting ideas and projects, you can anticipate any unauthorized access attempts and take immediate action to protect your assets. Whether someone is trying to access your files or steal your ideas, you will be armed with the knowledge and resources necessary to neutralize any potential threats and safeguard your innovation.

- **Security in online purchases:** Before making an online purchase, you can investigate the reputation of the website using cyber intelligence tools. This allows you to avoid falling into fraudulent or unsafe sites, thus protecting your personal and financial data.

When reading online opinions and product reviews, applying cyber intelligence techniques allows you to evaluate their authenticity. This helps you make informed decisions and avoid scams by identifying potential fake or manipulated reviews from untrustworthy sellers.

- **Digital identity control:** If you are concerned about the protection of your digital identity and online privacy, cyber intelligence serves as a tool for monitoring online profiles.

Start by setting up alerts about any suspicious activity or unauthorized changes to your social media profiles and other websites, login attempts, unusual locations or unknown devices, fake profiles, and more.

These basic cyber intelligence techniques will be very useful if you have to report the incident to the relevant authorities or take legal action as appropriate, including to track the IP address of the intruder and collect information about their online activities.

Books / movies and series - 60 key facts

[Intelligence Operations and Global Security]

BOOKS:

1. ***"Legacy of Ashes: The Story of the CIA"*** - Tim Weiner, 2007

The book "Legacy of Ashes: The History of the CIA" written by Tim Weiner, winner of the Pulitzer Prize in 2008, offers a comprehensive analysis of the development and actions of the Central Intelligence Agency (CIA) since its founding after the World War II until the events of September 11. Drawing on more than 50,000 declassified documents and interviews with numerous CIA veterans, Weiner provides a detailed and critical look at the agency.

Considered a fundamental work for understanding the second half of the 20th century, the book not only examines the operations, successes and failures of the CIA, but also its impact on world politics. It states that, despite the positive reputation maintained by the CIA, it has been marked by a series of serious errors that have been hidden in top secret files.

The author maintains that the initial mission of the CIA

was to understand the world and, if not achieved, to try to influence it. However, he notes that these attempts at change frequently resulted in significant failures. The book offers an insightful and revealing look at the world's most powerful intelligence agency and its impact on recent history. You can purchase the book on Amazon at this link: https://amzn.to/3VKSm09

2. **"Los Hombres de la Niebla"** – (The Men of the Fog) - Pablo Zarrabeitia, 2022

The Novel "Los Hombres de la Niebla" – written by an active agent of the National Intelligence Center (CNI) of Spain under a pseudonym, tells the intriguing story of a Spanish journalist who disappears in South America while investigating the traces of the former Nazi exile. This event triggers the global operation Wallachia by the Spanish CNI in an effort to find her.

The book offers an authentic and realistic view of the work of spies, highlighting the sacrifices, restrictions and constant tension they face in their lives. Through characters like Marcos Madero, the inner workings of the CNI are unraveled, exploring its procedures, operations and the daily lives of its agents.

With an immersive plot and compelling characters, the novel immerses the reader in a world of intrigue and danger, revealing the ins and outs of modern espionage and the challenges faced by those who practice it. "Los Hombres de la Niebla" is a captivating read that offers a fascinating look into the world of intelligence and covert action. It is available on Amazon at the link: https://amzn.to/3J1Danw

3. **"The Dark Agent: Memoirs of a spy infiltrated by the CNI"** – Anonymous et al., 2019

The book "The Dark Agent: Memoirs of a Spy Infiltrated by the

CNI" contains a fascinating story by an anonymous author who reveals his experiences as a Spanish spy infiltrated into the jihadist world by the National Intelligence Center (CNI). Through a first-person narrative, the text immerses the reader in the life of an apparent small businessman who, in reality, enters the world of Islamist radicals, travels with Muslim preachers and establishes contacts with Moroccan intelligence agents in Spain.

This work offers an immersive and realistic view of the field work of intelligence services, revealing the dangers, complexities and ethical dilemmas faced by undercover agents. In addition, it sheds light on the crucial work of Spanish counterespionage and reveals the pockets of Islamist radicalization that represent a threat to national security.

"The Dark Agent" provides a revealing look at the world of espionage and counterterrorism, showing the courage and dedication required to operate in the darkest corners of global conflict. It is available on Amazon at this link: https://amzn.to/3PL7Zkl

4. *"Inés y la Alegría"* - Almudena Grandes, 2010

The play "Inés y la Alegría" presents an interesting plot that revolves around the characters of Inés and Jesús Monzón, whose lives intertwine against a backdrop of secrecy and espionage during the summer of 1939 in Toulouse, France. Inés, a supporter of the republican cause during the Spanish civil war, lives in hiding under the surveillance of her brother, a provincial delegate of the Falange in Lérida.

Although Inés does not identify herself as a spy in the conventional sense, her participation in clandestine activities is suggested through her secret joy at clandestinely listening to the announcement of the "Reconquista de España" operation on Radio Pirenaica. This detail reveals her knowledge and possible involvement in covert events, adding a layer of intrigue and suspense to the plot.

The novel offers an insightful look at historical events and the complex web of personal relationships in a context of political and social conflict. Through the characters of Inés and Jesús, Almudena Grandes weaves a captivating story that explores themes of loyalty, identity and sacrifice in times of turbulence. It can be purchased on Amazon at this link: https://amzn.to/43WiA1P

5. *"How to Be a Spy"* - Daniel Nesquens, 2022

This new "How to Be a Spy" demystifies stereotypes about the world of espionage by stating that it is not necessary to be Russian, wear a trench coat or have an English mustache to become a true spy. Aimed at everyday people, but with a touch of instinct, this manual offers a complete guide that covers everything from what it is to be a spy to what essential techniques and gadgets to use, and even what to pack in your spy suitcase.

Throughout the book, younger readers will discover different types of spies, espionage techniques used in real life, as well as historical curiosities and a compilation of the best fictional spies. The work provides detailed advice, detailed descriptions and interactive activities, all presented with a perfect balance of humor, learning and playful illustrations.

Daniel Nesquens, an internationally acclaimed author with more than 40 books written, offers a unique and entertaining perspective on the fascinating world of espionage, inviting readers to immerse themselves in a journey full of intrigue and discovery. This manual is ideal to enjoy alone or in company, and you do not need to destroy it after reading it, unless you want to keep your own spy secrets! You can get it on Amazon at this secret link: https://amzn.to/3xvaf97

FILMS:

1. **"The 355"** – (USA, 2022)

   [International collaboration]

"The 355" brings together five rival female spies who come from different intelligence agencies. Despite their differences, they work together to confront a threat of a global cyber attack. Jessica Chastain, Diane Kruger, Lupita Nyong'o, Penélope Cruz and Fan Bingbing form a group called 355, in honor of the first female spy in the American Revolution. With an engaging cast, "Agents 355" offers important lessons in global security and intelligence operations, highlighting the need for international collaboration to confront digital threats and protect global stability. You can enjoy it on Amazon Prime Video and depending on your region, you could also get it on YouTube.

2. **"Topaz"** – (USA, 1969)

   [Infiltration of spy networks]

"Topaz" is an espionage thriller directed by Alfred Hitchcock, focusing on the Cuban missile crisis of 1962. Starring Frederick Stafford, Dany Robin, John Vernon and others, the film addresses the infiltration of a Soviet spy network in the United States during the Cold War, based on Leon 's novel of the same name Uris. The plot takes place in various settings around the world, including the United States, France and Cuba, and is full of unexpected twists, betrayals and intense tension. Set in a historical moment of great political and diplomatic instability, the film reflects the paranoia and distrust characteristic of the Cold War, offering an authentic vision of the world of espionage and exploring the complex ethical dilemmas faced by agents. Amazon Prime Video, Apple TV and other platforms have it in their catalog, but it is possible that it is available on YouTube.

3. **"Zero Dark Thirty"** - Darkest Night: Hunt for Osama Bin Laden (USA, 2012)

[Research and intelligence]

"Zero Dark Thirty" is generally considered the most accurate and insightful film in its depiction of the events leading up to the capture of Osama Bin Laden. Unlike "Code Geronimo" which focuses on the capture operation, this one focuses on the character of Maya, played by Jessica Chastain, a CIA agent, and her tireless dedication to locating Bin Laden. After years of arduous investigation, including interrogations with torture in Afghanistan, Maya finally achieves success with the military operation that ended the life of Al-Qaeda leader Osama Bin Laden in Abbottabad, Pakistan, on May 2, 2011, a moment known as "Zero Dark Thirty". The film highlights the importance of individual work and the ability of a single person to make a difference in the complex world of intelligence, highlighting how Maya's determination and unique vision were critical to the mission's success, even after almost a decade since the 9/11 attacks, it has been available on almost all platforms, including Netflix, Amazon Prime Video, Hulu, Google Play Movies, Google TV, Microsoft Movies and TV, Vudu, Rakuten and even YouTube.

4. **"Black Book"** – (HOL, 2006)

[Infiltrate agent]

"Black Book" originally "Zwartboek" is a drama that takes place during World War II in the Netherlands occupied by German troops. The story follows Rachel Stein, a young Jewish woman played by Carice van Houten, who, after losing her family to the Nazis, joins the Resistance. Their dangerous mission is to infiltrate Nazi Headquarters and seduce a high-ranking German officer to obtain vital information that could save their captured comrades. The film presents a mix of drama, intrigue and action in a tense historical context, where Rachel faces moral dilemmas and challenges as she fights for freedom and justice in the midst of war. Enjoy it on Rakuten TV, Google TV or

Amazon Prime Video

5. *"Notorious"* – (USA, 1946)

[Romance in spy operations]

"Notorious", directed by Alfred Hitchcock and starring Ingrid Bergman and Cary Grant, tells the story of Alicia, daughter of a Nazi spy, who becomes romantically involved with a US government agent to infiltrate a group of Nazis refugees in Brazil. As Alicia and Devlin deepen their relationship, they face emotional challenges and physical dangers as they try to unravel Nazi conspiracies. The plot thickens when Alicia is forced to marry one of the conspirators to gather information for the government. "Bounded" is a classic of American film noir, recognized for its outstanding performances, masterful direction by Hitchcock and a tense, immersive narrative. Depending on your location, you could find it on Amazon Prime Video, Netflix, Hulu, Google TV, Apple TV or YouTube, but you can also check platforms like FilmAffinity, JustWatch, FullTV to check where it's available in your country.

SERIES:

1. *"October Missiles"* – (USA, 1974)

[2 Episodes | 1 Season]

The series "October Missiles" is a docudrama in miniseries format that was broadcast in 1974. It is a historical and dramatic exploration of one of the most dangerous episodes in modern history. It is based on the Cuban missile crisis during the Cold War. The title refers to Barbara Tuchman's book, "The Guns of August", which explores the mistakes of great powers and failed opportunities to give an opponent a graceful exit, ultimately leading to World War I.

The production is dazzling, it won several awards. The script is based on Robert Kennedy's book, "Thirteen Days: Memoirs of the Cuban Missile Crisis", published posthumously in 1969.

Focusing on the 13 days in which the world was on the brink of a nuclear war between States United States and the Soviet Union, the series shows the political and military tension surrounding the crisis, as well as the decisions made by US President John F. Kennedy and his administration to avoid a catastrophic conflict in 1962. Depending on your location, it is It is possible to find it on some streaming platforms, series libraries of some cable television channels. On the Archive.org website you can play and download an English version, subtitled, for free.

2. *"Spy Wars"* - War Spies | War Spies (UK, 2019)

[8 Episodes | 1 Season]

"Spy Wars" is a British series hosted by Damian Lewis, known for his roles in "Billions" and "Homeland". In each chapter, it reveals the true story behind the most shocking secret missions in history. Through innovative reconstructions and expert testimony, intriguing cases of international espionage from the Cold War to the present day are explored.

The production, recorded in London, Moscow and Israel, reveals notorious details of emblematic events, including the escape of American diplomats from Tehran, which was also reflected in the film "Argo", the case of the former Russian military intelligence officer who survived an attempted murder with nerve gas in 2018 or the largest surveillance operation in British history. If you are interested in the world of espionage and international conspiracies, this proposal will captivate you. Depending on your region, you can get it on RTVE, Amazon Prime Video, Apple TV, Netflix, HBO Max, documentary websites or YouTube, but on Documaniatv.com it is available for free and in Spanish.

3. *"The Night Manager"* – (UK/USA, 2016)

[6 Episodes | 1 Season]

"The Night Manager" is a British-American miniseries based

on the internationally acclaimed novel by master writer John le Carré. The plot follows Jonathan Pine, a former soldier who becomes the night manager at a luxury hotel. He soon becomes embroiled in a world of espionage and corruption when he is asked to act as an informant for the British government to infiltrate the inner circle of a dangerous arms dealer and drug dealer. The series is full of intrigue, suspense and unexpected twists as Pine navigates a world of deception and danger.

"The Night Manager" received 36 nominations and multiple awards, being highly acclaimed by critics and the public for its script, performances and high-quality production. Since late 2016, Amazon Prime Video acquired the streaming rights to this series for 180 countries, so there's a good chance it will be available in your location.

4. **"Mrs. Wilson"** – (UK, 2018)

[3 Episodes | 1 Season]

"Mrs. Wilson" is a British miniseries based on true events that follows the story of Alison Wilson. After the death of her husband, Alec Wilson, Alison discovers that he had multiple wives and secret families. The series explores the secrets and lies of Alec, an MI6 agent, and how it affects Alison and her children as they try to discover the truth about his life and marriage. It is inspired by the extraordinary story of actress Ruth Wilson's own grandparents.

You can enjoy "Mrs. Wilson" on various streaming platforms depending on your location. Some options could include Amazon Prime Video, Apple TV, Netflix, BBC iPlayer or video on demand services offering BBC content.

5. **"Carmen Sandiego"** (USA, 2016)

[33 Episodes | 4 Seasons]

"Carmen Sandiego" is an animated Netflix series that

combines action, adventure and educational elements, addressing themes of justice, morality and redemption. The plot follows Carmen, a cunning thief turned vigilante, who travels the world unraveling crimes and robberies like a kind of modern-day Robin Hood. Their goal is to thwart the plans of the evil organization VILE and protect artifacts of great historical and cultural value from being used for nefarious purposes. Despite her noble cause, Carmen Sandiego is perceived as a criminal by most law enforcement agencies, including INTERPOL and a mysterious organization called ACME.

You can see this modern version of "Carmen Sandiego" on the Netflix streaming platform. You can also find the 1994 production, "Where on Earth Is Carmen Sandiego", known as "In Search of Carmen Sandiego" or "Where in the World is Carmen Sandiego?", with 40 episodes, inspired by the famous educational video game from the 80s developed by Brøderbund Software.

In our exploration, we have uncovered the invisible work of intelligence agencies that sustain global security. These entities are essential to anticipate and neutralize threats, from terrorist attacks to human-induced natural disasters, thus protecting our lives and social stability.

Thanks to their efforts, we can live with peace of mind, travel with confidence and enjoy a stable economic environment. Through strategic counterespionage, counterterrorism and cyber intelligence operations, these agencies ensure our security at all levels.

In today's digital age, where information crosses borders easily, counterespionage, counterterrorism and cyber intelligence have become relevant terms not only for government agencies, but also in our daily lives. Just as nations protect their secrets, we too must be cautious in safeguarding our personal information from unauthorized access, underscoring the importance of data security in our daily lives.

By following the recommendations in this chapter and maintaining a vigilant attitude, both in daily life and in your family environment, you can strengthen your security and minimize the risk of being a victim of intrusions, fraud or privacy violations.

To better understand Intelligence operations and global security, I encourage you to watch a movie or series from the list of recommendations on this topic. Then, share your thoughts and comments with me at www.mujersecurity.com. Your perspective is invaluable and will contribute to the dialogue about the safety and well-being of our people.

CHAPTER 4: CHALLENGES, CONTROVERSIES AND ETHICAL DILEMMAS

Facing a constantly evolving landscape, the modern era poses ethical, legal and operational challenges for entities charged with national security. These bodies must carefully navigate between the protection of state interests and respect for the rights and privacy of individuals. Legally, they are forced to adapt to technological innovations and emerging threats, which involves continuous re-evaluation of laws and the formulation of new policies.

From an operational point of view, technological innovation is essential to counter cyber threats and terrorism, but it must be done without undermining public trust or the legitimacy of actions taken. The era of big data and artificial intelligence accelerates technological development, often exceeding the capacity of institutional response. Furthermore, differences in legislation and ethical standards between countries can complicate international collaboration, vital to addressing threats that do not respect borders.

This chapter explores the ethical dilemmas and legal controversies arising from mass surveillance, as well as the compelling need to balance transparency, accountability, and confidentiality. This trio is essential to preserving both operational effectiveness and public trust in a period marked by rapid and significant change.

Innovative methods in intelligence management

In the dynamic scenario of national and global security, intelligence agencies face increasingly complex and sophisticated challenges. To address this changing reality, governments have ushered in a new era of innovative methods and advanced technology.

From the application of artificial intelligence to big data analytics and facial recognition, these revolutionary tools have not only transformed the way information is collected and analyzed but have also redefined the boundaries of what is possible in the intelligence field. In the following pages, I will reveal how these innovations are boosting the ability of intelligence agencies to meet the challenges of the 21st century and protect the security and well-being of nations and their citizens.

Artificial Intelligence (AI): The impact of artificial intelligence (AI) on the operations of intelligence agencies is undeniable. As Yuval points out Atsmon, senior partner at the McKinsey Center for Strategic Innovation in London, AI is transforming not only current strategies, but also what is to come. And for the operations of intelligence agencies it has become a fundamental pillar, allowing large amounts of data to be processed quickly and efficiently, identifying patterns and trends that may go unnoticed by human analysts.

Let's see how AI benefits and makes the work of intelligence personnel easier:

- **Data analysis at scale:** AI makes it possible to analyze large volumes of data including intercepted communications, financial records, satellite images and social media posts. This approach allows relevant

information and potential threats to be identified in a precise and timely manner.
- **Pattern Recognition:** With machine learning algorithms, AI identifies patterns and irregular behaviors in data. This is crucial to prevent terrorist attacks, uncover smuggling networks and dismantle criminal organizations.
- **Automation of repetitive tasks:** Routine and monotonous tasks, such as document classification and language translation. This automation frees up analysts' time and talent, allowing them to focus on more complex and strategic tasks.
- **Prediction and anticipation:** AI enables the anticipation of future events, such as political crises or outbreaks of violence, by identifying patterns and correlations in data. This capacity allows preventive measures to be taken with the aim of mitigating its impact.

Artificial intelligence has become a powerful tool to improve the efficiency, operational capabilities and security of intelligence agencies in an increasingly complex and dynamic environment, on a global scale.

Facial recognition: An innovative method that is revolutionizing the security and efficiency of intelligence agency operations by allowing accurate identification of individuals in images or videos. This technology relies on machine learning algorithms that examine distinctive facial features and compare them with databases of previously registered faces.

Intelligence agencies use facial recognition in a wide range of areas:
- **Identification of people:** Facial recognition allows people to be identified in real time or from previously

captured images and videos. This is useful for identifying suspects in public places, airports, train stations, among others.
- **Surveillance and monitoring:** Intelligence agencies can use facial recognition systems to monitor areas of interest and detect the presence of wanted individuals or individuals of national security interest.
- **Criminal Investigations:** In criminal investigations, facial recognition can help link individuals to criminal activities, identify accomplices, or determine the presence of key people in certain locations at specific times.
- **Border security:** At points of entry and exit into the country, such as airports and land borders, facial recognition is used to verify the identity of travelers and detect possible threats or people on watch lists.
- **Intelligence analysis:** Facial recognition is also used in intelligence analysis to identify connections between individuals, track movements and activities, and gather information about criminal or terrorist networks. Without a doubt, this technology is a multifaceted tool that is very useful in both the intelligence and commercial fields, and even in mobile telephony.

From its application to locate missing people, identify suspects or control access in public places, to its use to personalize customer experiences, recommend products based on facial profiles or improve service in stores and services, this technology is innovating in customer satisfaction.

Furthermore, in the context of mobile telephony, facial recognition has been integrated into the biometric authentication of devices, improving security and user experience in accessing sensitive data and mobile applications. With its increasing development and adoption, facial recognition promises to continue transforming various aspects of our lives, from security to consumer experience, in an increasingly interconnected and digitalized future.

Big data analytics: With the exponential growth of digitally generated data, intelligence agencies are faced with the challenge of extracting valuable and relevant information from this overwhelming amount of information. Big data analysis becomes another innovative method of great relevance for intelligence operations.

By applying advanced algorithms and data mining techniques, patterns, trends and relationships that could go unnoticed by human analysts are identified. This approach provides them with a more complete and in-depth view of potential threats, criminal behavior and the movements of suspicious actors, helping them make more informed and proactive decisions regarding national and global security.

Here are some key aspects of how big data is used in this context:

- **Big data analytics:** Social media generates huge amounts of data every day in the form of posts, comments, messages, and user profiles. Big data (according to the RAE) allows intelligence agencies to collect, store and analyze this data on a large scale to identify significant patterns, trends and behaviors.
- **Real-time processing:** Big data facilitates rapid processing of large volumes of data in real time. This is crucial for continuous monitoring of social media for suspicious activity or emerging trends that may require an immediate response from authorities.
- **Identification of connections and networks:** By analyzing data on social networks through Big Data techniques, intelligence agencies can identify connections between individuals, groups and organizations. This allows them to map networks of influence, identify leaders and followers,

and understand the structure and dynamics of extremist groups or other suspicious entities.

- **Detection of anomalies and unusual behavior:** Big Data allows intelligence agencies to use advanced algorithms to detect anomalies and unusual behavior in social media data. This may include sudden changes in activity patterns, the spread of false information, or the appearance of hate speech, all of which may be indicative of suspicious activity.

This enhances the ability to gather information more efficiently in a constantly evolving threat environment and address complex national and global security challenges. However, its implementation also raises important ethical and privacy issues, such as access to content, which must be addressed with caution and responsibility.

Big data and data analysis

In an increasingly connected world, the amount of data generated daily is colossal, like a constantly growing ocean. Who is tasked with navigating these vast waters of information? This is where intelligence agencies come into play.

Imagine that you are planning your next trip. You open your browser and search for destinations, flights, hotels and activities. Every click, every search, leaves a digital footprint. These seemingly simple actions are part of big data, that vast ocean of information made up of structured and unstructured data that constantly flows through the network.

Now, how does this relate to intelligence agencies and their daily work? Well... let's say you are an analyst at an agency in charge of national security. Your mission is to detect possible threats and prevent attacks. How do you do it? Using data analysis, of course. You observe behavioral patterns on social media, analyze electronic communications, and monitor suspicious financial transactions. All of this is part of the vast field of open-source intelligence, where big data becomes your most powerful ally.

But here's the key: big data alone is just the first sip of coffee; Data analysis is the process that turns that sip into a full cup, rich in information and understanding. Thanks to data analysis, usually in open sources such as social networks, intelligence agencies can detect trends, identify emerging threats and make informed decisions in real time.

Metadata and big data: Similarities and differences

In an increasingly connected world, the concepts of metadata and big data are essential to navigate the vast ocean of digital information that surrounds us. Both play a crucial role in understanding and harnessing this abundance of data, and their relevance extends to even our simplest daily activities. In this text, we will explore the similarities and differences between these two concepts, and how intelligence agencies use this information to protect and serve society.

Metadata is like "data about data". They provide context and organization to digital information, allowing it to be easily retrieved and understood. For example, when we send an email, the attached metadata may include details such as the date, time, sender, and recipient of the message. Similarly, a digital photograph may be accompanied by metadata describing the location and time it was taken, as well as the camera used. This metadata is essential to understand the context of the data and facilitate its efficient management.

On the other hand, big data refers to extremely large and complex data sets that challenge the capabilities of traditional database tools. This data can be structured, such as enterprise databases, or unstructured, such as social media posts, emails, or videos. Big data is characterized by its volume, speed and variety, making it an invaluable source of information and knowledge.

Both metadata and big data They are vital tools for Intelligence

Agencies in the collection and analysis of information. Metadata allows them to track and contextualize digital communication, while big data provides a broader view of the patterns and trends within this data. This information is essential for detecting threats and making informed decisions regarding national security.

In conclusion, metadata and big data They are two sides of the same coin in the digital world. Both are essential to understanding and harnessing digital information, and intelligence agencies play a crucial role in managing and analyzing it to protect and serve society as a whole.

So the next time you browse the web, remember that every click can have an impact on the security of all of us. Big data is a powerful tool, and thanks to data analysis, our intelligence agencies are working to protect us, even in the digital world. And while you're at it, why not enjoy a cup of coffee or your favorite beverage and reflect on the power of information in our lives?

Books / movies and series - 60 key facts

[Challenges and controversies]

BOOKS:

1. **"The Looming Tower: Al-Qaeda and the Road to 9/11"** - Lawrence Wright, 2006

In "The Looming Tower: Al-Qaeda and the Road to 9/11" Pulitzer Prize-winning Lawrence Wright delves into the internal conflict between American intelligence agencies, especially the FBI and the CIA. Through exhaustive research, the author examines how rivalry and lack of cooperation between these agencies affected their ability to prevent the attacks of September 11, 2001. The lack of coordination resulted in missed opportunities to anticipate and prevent the devastating attack to the Twin Towers.

According to the newspaper El País, this book is considered

the best work on Osama bin Laden, his relationship with Ayman al-Zawahiri and the events of 9/11. Wright's meticulous research offers an illuminating and critical insight into the origins and development of one of the most shocking events in modern history. Its relevance continues to resonate in the global political and security arena, highlighting the importance of effective cooperation and coordination between intelligence agencies.

This work provides a penetrating look at the complex landscape of US national security, highlighting the challenges and consequences of institutional rivalry in the fight against international terrorism. Their approach reveals the systemic failures that allowed 9/11 to occur, providing a valuable lesson about the importance of collaboration and information sharing in preventing future attacks. Available on Amazon at the following link: https://amzn.to/3TYFsZZ

2. ***"Data and Goliath: The Hidden Battles to Collect Your Data and Control Your World"*** - Bruce Schneier, 2016

In this work, Schneier, a recognized security expert, uncovers the extensive network of surveillance, censorship and propaganda that prevails in contemporary society. Explores the dangers of cybercrime, cyberterrorism, and cyberwar, and proposes technological, legal, and social solutions to forge a more equitable, private, and secure world.

The author examines how our personal data is generated as a natural byproduct of our online activity and examines how it is collected by both companies and governments. Additionally, it explores the impact of surveillance on our political freedoms and rights, offering recommendations for both government and corporate entities. It also provides practical tips for users to protect their privacy in their daily lives.

"Data and Goliath" is essential reading for those who

want to understand the complexity of the digital age and the implications of massive data collection on our society. Available on Amazon, this book provides an informed and insightful view on a topic of vital importance in the contemporary world. Available in English on Amazon https://amzn.to/49i9SvL

3. *"Corazón tan Blanco"* - A Heart So White | Javier Marías, 1999

"Corazón tan Blanco" by Javier Marías, published in 1999, has left an indelible mark on world literature. Published in 44 countries and translated into 37 languages, with more than 2,300,000 copies sold worldwide, the novel has been awarded internationally and has received praise from both critics and readers in various linguistic fields. It is, without a doubt, a contemporary classic that endures over time.

Although not specifically a work about espionage or intelligence, "Heart So White" offers universal lessons that transcend the boundaries of the genre. The protagonist, mistaking an unknown woman for his intended date, reminds us of the importance of close observation and caution, as experienced in the world of espionage. In this environment, the most valuable information often lies in what is not said and appearances can be deceptive.

Marías' ability to weave a complex and captivating plot, full of intrigue and suspense, leads us to reflect on human nature and the complexity of interpersonal relationships. "Heart So White" not only entertains us, but also invites us to look beyond superficial appearances and explore the hidden depths of the human mind and heart. It can be found on Amazon https://amzn.to/3VYjn0f

4. *"Galloping Spies"* - Berry Bees Book, 2020

In "Galloping Spies", our intrepid mini spies engage in a

horse-riding competition to unravel the mystery behind a suspicious fire. It's an enigma that only these astute agents will be able to solve.

The Berry Bees series, devised by Carolina Capria and Maria Martucci, aka Cat Le Blanc, is an Italian creation made up of six titles to date. The plot follows Lola, Bobby and Juliette, a trio of girls with extraordinary abilities, a strong friendship and a secret life as Berry Bees agents at the BIA (Bees Intelligence Agency), led by the mysterious Mrs. Berry. With skills in hacking systems, reading minds, and unparalleled agility, these young women are sent on missions that adult agents cannot undertake. Although not yet translated into English, the books have been translated into multiple languages, including Spanish, Catalan, Portuguese, and others.

The series includes exciting titles such as Three Spies for a Miss, Mission Gold Collar and Danger in Paris, offering a captivating blend of adventure, intrigue and friendship. Additionally, the books have inspired an animated series that premiered in Australia in October 2019. If you're a fan of exciting adventures and mysteries, the Berry Bees books are sure to keep you captivated! And you can get them on Amazon https://amzn.to/4cIDLZ7

> 5. **"I was the spy who loved the Commander: A movie life: from the Nazi camps to Fidel Castro, the CIA and Kennedy's assassin"** - Marita: The Spy Who Loved Castro| Marita Lorenz, 2015

In her book "I was the Spy who Loved the Commander", Marita Lorenz narrates a life marked by turbulence and intrigue from her first days in Germany in 1939, in the midst of the chaos of the invasion of Poland. Daughter of a captain of German ship and an American actress, Marita experienced the horror of the Bergen-Belsen concentration camp during her childhood, where she was also a victim of violence at a young age.

Her sea voyages with her father took her to Havana in 1959, where a chance meeting with Fidel Castro sparked a passionate relationship that made her his lover at the young age of nineteen. However, her relationship with Castro was soon overshadowed by betrayal and pain when the CIA convinced her that he was responsible for the loss of her baby, leading to a failed attempt to assassinate him.

Returning to Miami, Marita crossed paths with prominent figures such as former Venezuelan dictator Marcos Pérez Jiménez and became involved in the political and social tumult of the time. Her connection to the convoy that included Lee Harvey Oswald before Kennedy's assassination in 1963 and her involvement in the world of the New York mafia add layers of mystery and danger to her story. Available on Amazon at this link: https://amzn.to/49wIzxP

FILMS:

1. **"Deciphering Enigma"** - The Imitation Game (USA, 2014)

[Ethical consequences]

"Deciphering Enigma", also known as "The Imitation Game ", is a 2014 film that tells the true story of Alan Turing, played by Benedict Cumberbatch, and his team during World War II, who worked to crack the codes of the Enigma machine used by German forces. Although it is not A typical spy movie, it addresses issues of intelligence, secrets, and personal sacrifice in the secret service. Technological innovation, teamwork, information security, ethical consequences, and making difficult decisions are key lessons learned. intelligence agencies can learn from this film. These lessons are still relevant in the modern world, where technology, ethics and information security are fundamental in the field of intelligence. You can find it on major streaming platforms such as Amazon. Prime Video, Google TV, Apple TV, Netflix or HBO Max and depending on your region, maybe YouTube you can get it for free in Spanish and in high resolution on PlutoTV.

2. **"Malavita"** - The Family | A Dangerous Family (USA, 2013)

[Protected informant]

"The Family", also known as "Malavita", is an American film that follows the story of the Manzoni family, led by Giovanni Manzoni, a former mobster who now works as an FBI informant. To protect his family, they are transferred to a picturesque village in Normandy, France, where they try to live a normal life under new names. However, violence and problems from the past haunt them and the family faces dangerous situations as they try to adapt to their new life with a stellar cast that includes. starring Robert De Niro, Michelle Pfeiffer and Tommy Lee Jones, this thriller offers an intriguing combination of drama, action and suspense. It is available in Spanish on PlutoTV.

3. **"Spies in Disguise"** – (USA, 2019)

[Adaptability]

"Spies in Disguise" is an animated action comedy, starring Will Smith as superspy Lance Sterling, who, after being accidentally transformed into a pigeon, is forced to work with a young inventor, played by Tom Holland. Together, they must join forces to stop a villain and save the world. The film addresses themes of teamwork, acceptance of differences and the importance of emotional intelligence in conflict situations. Disney Plus, Apple TV and Google TV are good options to get it.

4. **"Salt"** - (USA, 2010)

[Internal security]

With the threat of an impending catastrophe dubbed "X-Day" and a plot to assassinate the Russian president, Evelyn Salt, a CIA agent, is forced to go on the run and use her skills to avoid capture and clear her name. "Salt" offers an intriguing look at the possibility of double agents within an organization. The plot stimulates a reflection on the need to review and strengthen security mechanisms to protect against internal threats. With its breakneck pace and focus on loyalty, betrayal and survival, the film captivates viewers who enjoy thrilling stories of espionage and suspense. You can watch it on Movistar Plus, Apple TV, Amazon Prime Video and other platforms.

5. **"Get Smart"** – (USA, 2008)

[Technology and Gadgets]

In "Get Smart", a 2008 spy comedy based on the 1960s television series "Get Smart", Steve Carell plays Maxwell Smart, a bumbling intelligence analyst who longs to become a field agent. When the headquarters of the CONTROL Spy Agency is attacked, Smart is given the opportunity to prove himself on a mission to stop the plans of the terrorist organization KAOS and save the world, along with Agent 99, played by Anne Hathaway. The film offers a mix of action and comedy, making it an entertaining option to watch with the family.

SERIES:

1. **"Counterpart"** - Parallel Lives (USA, 2016)

[20 Episodes | 2 Seasons]

"Counterpart", known as "Parallel Lives", is a television series that combines elements of science fiction and espionage. The plot follows Howard Silk, a low-level employee at a UN bureaucratic body in Berlin, who discovers that his organization is hiding access to a parallel dimension. In this other world, Howard meets his counterpart, a man identical to him, but with a very different life and personality.

As the series progresses, Howard becomes embroiled in a world of intrigue, conspiracies and secrets involving both realities, realizing that he can only trust one person: his "other self" from another dimension. The series explores themes such as identity, morality and the consequences of our decisions, offering unexpected twists and complex character development. "Vidas Paralelas" provides a captivating television experience for lovers of science fiction and suspense, and is available to watch on Movistar Plus and Amazon Prime Video.

2. **"Berlin Station"** – (USA, 2016)

[29 Episodes | 3 Seasons]

"Berlin Station" is an exciting drama that follows Daniel Meyer, a CIA agent who is forced to move to Berlin with a clandestine mission. His objective is to discover the origin of a leak about a mole or snitch within the agency who has Provided information to a whistleblower known only as "Thomas Shaw". Daniel soon learns to deal with the violent and harsh world of field agent work, as well as the deceptions, dangers, and moral compromises.

"Berlin Station" shows the interiors of a CIA station in a European capital, addressing issues of international politics, corruption and betrayal, underscoring the importance of surveillance and security in an increasingly interconnected world. You can watch it on Epix, Amazon Prime Video or Apple TV, SkyShowtime, Movistar Plus and other platforms, depending on your region.

3. **"Covert Affairs"** – (USA, 2010)

[75 Episodes | 5 Seasons]

A polyglot young CIA trainee, Annie Walker, is sent to work in the Domestic Protection Division (DPD), where she serves as a field agent. August "Auggie" Anderson, a blind tech agent, is Annie's guide in her new life. Annie's cover is that she works in the Acquisitions department at the Smithsonian Museum.

"Covert Affairs" is distinguished from other intelligence and espionage series by its strong female protagonist, whose journey from rookie to seasoned agent is intertwined with her personal and romantic life, as well as by the inclusion of an agent character blind, challenging the traditional stereotypes of this genre, offering a more diverse narrative and emotionally resonant compared to other series in the genre. You can watch it on SkyShowtime, Amazon Prime Video, Apple TV, Peacock and other platforms, depending on your region.

4. **"Killing Eve"** – (USA, 2018)

[24 Episodes | 4 Seasons]

"Killing Eve" is a spy drama based on the novels by Luke Jennings. The plot centers on the intense mutual obsession between a resourceful MI6 agent whose boring job strays from her dream of being a spy and a ruthless and elegant psychopathic assassin. Throughout the series, both women face off in a game of cat and mouse that takes them across Europe and other parts of the world.

The series stands out for its exploration of the complex psychology of the characters, its unexpected tone of dark humor and its fresh approach to themes of identity, morality and the nature of evil, offering an exciting and unique experience in the spy thriller genre. It is available on BBC America, AMC, Hulu, BBC iPlayer, HBO Max, Amazon Prime Video and other local streaming platforms.

5. **"KC Undercover"** – (USA, 2015)

[77 Episodes | 3 Seasons]

"KC Undercover" is a comedy-action series that follows the

adventures of a teenage math student who discovers that her parents are secret spies. As she delves deeper into the world of espionage, KC becomes an agent in training and must balance her everyday life as a high school student with her secret missions to save the world.

The series is full of humor, action and family moments while facing exciting spy adventures. You can enjoy it on Disney Channel and Disney+ and other streaming platforms, depending on your region and available streaming options.

The landscape of challenges, controversies, and ethical dilemmas facing intelligence agencies in the modern era is vast and complex. From the rapid evolution of technology to the imperative of balancing national security with individual rights, these entities are at a crucial crossroads in preserving the stability and well-being of societies.

Innovative methods in intelligence management, such as artificial intelligence, facial recognition and big data analysis, represent a leap forward in the ability of intelligence agencies to address emerging threats. However, this progress is not without controversies and ethical dilemmas. Mass surveillance, access to personal data and transparency are hot topics that require a delicate balance between security and privacy.

In this context, international collaboration becomes increasingly vital to address threats that transcend national borders. However, differences in legislation and ethical standards may hinder this joint effort, underscoring the need for a global and coordinated approach to ensure safety in an interconnected world.

Ultimately, the key lies in finding a balance between technological innovation, protecting national security and respect for individual rights. Transparency, accountability, and respect for privacy are critical to preserving public trust and the legitimacy of actions taken by intelligence agencies.

To delve deeper into this topic and better understand the challenges and opportunities that intelligence agencies face, I recommend watching a movie or series that I have selected to recommend to you. Afterwards, I invite you to share your reflections on your social networks, where you can interact with me and find other content that I have published on my website, YouTube, Spotify and the main social networks with the user @mujerseguridad.

CHAPTER 5: INTELLIGENCE, TRANSPARENCY AND ACCOUNTABILITY

Intelligence agencies have enormous power and capacity to influence the lives of citizens and the course of events on a national and international scale. Therefore, it is essential that they operate transparently and take responsibility for their actions. Transparency allows society to better understand the activities of these agencies, ensuring that their actions are aligned with democratic values and human rights.

Accountability, on the other hand, ensures that intelligence agencies are accountable to the public and democratic institutions for their actions and decisions. This includes oversight by the legislature, judiciary, and other oversight institutions, as well as the ability to investigate and correct any abuse or misconduct by these agencies.

Transparency and accountability are fundamental principles for any institution that wields significant power, and intelligence agencies are no exception. Operating with transparency means that these agencies must communicate their methods and operations within limits that do not compromise national security or ongoing operations. Responsibility for your actions is equally crucial; They must justify their operations and take responsibility for any consequences that arise from their actions.

These principles not only strengthen public trust in intelligence agencies, but also serve as a check on the power these entities possess. In a world where privacy is increasingly threatened by technology and data collection, it is vital that intelligence agencies adhere to high ethical standards and are subject to oversight and control.

Transparency and accountability are also important for the democratic functioning of a society. They allow citizens to be informed and provide the basis for public debate and policy formulation. In addition, they help prevent abuses of power and ensure that intelligence agencies operate for the benefit of society and not to its detriment.

To improve transparency and accountability in the work of intelligence agencies, a number of measures can be implemented. One of them is to strengthen supervision and control mechanisms, guaranteeing that there are independent bodies in charge of monitoring the activities of these agencies and investigating any irregularities or abuse.

Another proposal is to promote a culture of transparency and openness within the intelligence agencies themselves, encouraging the proactive disclosure of relevant information to the public and facilitating access to data on their operations and decisions. This may include publishing annual reports, participating in public hearings, and collaborating with civil society organizations and the media.

Furthermore, it is important to strengthen the legal and regulatory mechanisms that govern the work of intelligence agencies, ensuring that there are clear and proportional sanctions for those who violate the law or abuse their power. This may include reviewing and updating intelligence laws, as well as creating independent oversight committees and implementing safeguards to protect the individual rights and privacy of citizens.

In this fifth chapter, we reflect on the importance of intelligence agencies operating transparently and taking responsibility for their actions, as well as proposals to improve transparency and accountability in their work. Throughout this book, we will continue to explore the complex world of intelligence agencies and their impact on our society and the international order.

Power is not unlimited and intelligence agencies know it

German Chancellor Angela Merkel and then-Brazilian President Dilma Rousseff publicly denounced the mass surveillance practices revealed by Edward Snowden, highlighting international concern over the violation of privacy in the monitoring of electronic communications.

Intelligence agencies understand that power is not unlimited. However, they can abuse their electronic communications monitoring powers to spy on innocent citizens, political dissidents, journalists and activists, in order to quell opposition and maintain political control. This undermines public trust in government institutions and threatens the rule of law. This awareness of the limits of power is essential to maintaining the balance between national security and respect for privacy and civil rights.

Now, I propose another coffee break, because this point deserves a closer look. I will share with you concrete case examples that will help you better understand how electronic communications monitoring impacts our lives. From scandals that have shaken the world to reports of everyday situations of abuse of power. Through concrete examples, I hope to show you the complexity of this topic and how it affects us in our daily lives. Do you already have your cup ready? Here we go!

Let's start with the most emblematic case, the Watergate scandal, in which agents of President Nixon's administration carried out an illegal raid on the headquarters of the Democratic Party National Committee in the Watergate building in Washington DC, with the purpose of obtaining information about the political strategies of his Democratic rivals during the United States presidential elections in 1972.

In 2017, it was revealed that the Mexican government had used controversial spy *software* known as "Project Pegasus" to spy on journalists, human rights activists, and political opponents, sparking widespread protests and criticism over abuse of power and rape. of privacy.

The US NSA has also been accused of spying on world leaders such as Angela Merkel, François Hollande and Dilma Rousseff, generating significant diplomatic tensions and calling into question the security of diplomatic communications.

Some claim that Israel's powerful Mossad spied on leaders such as US Secretary of State John Kerry during peace negotiations between Israel and Palestine, raising concerns about the security of diplomatic communications between Israel and the United States.

Russia has been accused of espionage against leaders such as François Hollande and Angela Merkel, increasing tensions between Russia and several European countries and raising concerns about the security of diplomatic communications.

In Latin America there have also been cases of scandals involving spying on electronic communications of heads of state and political leaders. In addition to the president of Brazil, Dilma Rousseff and her predecessor, Luiz Inácio Lula da Silva, in Brazil; In 2013, it was revealed that NSA may have intercepted the electronic communications of then-Mexican President Enrique Peña Nieto and other high-level Mexican officials.

This scandal caused a serious diplomatic crisis between the United States and Mexico, and generated great concern about the privacy of communications in the region. This case exemplifies how espionage of electronic communications can have significant repercussions on bilateral relations between countries and trust between governments.

More recently, the Brazilian Intelligence Agency (ABIN) has been embroiled in an illegal spying scandal against political rivals and journalists during President Jair Bolsonaro's term. Brazil's Federal Police claims that using a computer program known as FirstMile, the agency was able to track the movements of up to 10,000 people every twelve months without following any official protocol. All that was needed was to digitize his phone number to carry out these surveillance activities.

Revelations by Edward Snowden indicated that the NSA had been spying on the communications of Chinese leaders, including President Xi Jinping, sparking condemnation from the Chinese government and tensions in bilateral relations with the United States.

These are just a few examples of cases where privacy violations have occurred in the monitoring of electronic communications, underscoring the importance of establishing appropriate safeguards and controls to protect individuals' civil rights and privacy.

Electronic communications monitoring: The good, the beautiful and the ugly

Although this may raise privacy concerns, electronic communications monitoring plays a crucial role in protecting national security and the well-being of citizens. Intelligence agencies employ sophisticated surveillance techniques to identify and prevent threats, from terrorism to cybercrime. In this context, it is important to understand both the benefits and ethical challenges associated with these practices, as well as their impact on our daily lives.

From texting to online shopping, your daily activities leave a digital trail that can be monitored and analyzed. That is why I show you, without any warm words, the good, the beautiful and the ugly of monitoring electronic communications, so that you take it into account in each cyber interaction and think carefully about the consequences of your actions "before the *click*."

The good

Threat prevention: Monitoring electronic communications can be an effective tool to prevent terrorist activities, cyberattacks, transnational crimes, and other threats to national security. By analyzing large volumes of data, intelligence agencies can identify patterns and early warning signals that could indicate planning criminal actions. There are countless cases in which monitoring electronic communications has been essential to prevent threats. Surely, some of the following examples will be familiar to you:

- **The Boston Bombing:** After the Boston Marathon bombing in 2013, it was discovered that the perpetrators, the Tsarnaev brothers, had exchanged jihadist messages on the internet before the attack. Monitoring electronic communications allowed authorities to track and disrupt other possible attack plans.

- **The plot to assassinate Queen Elizabeth II:** In 2014, British intelligence intercepted electronic communications between suspects planning to assassinate Queen Elizabeth II during a memorial ceremony in London. Thanks to the monitoring of these communications, arrests were made and the attack was prevented.

- **The terrorist plot in Australia:** In 2017, Australian intelligence agencies thwarted a terrorist plot involving a plan to blow up a plane. Monitoring electronic communications was crucial to identifying the plotters and preventing the planned attack.

These cases highlight how electronic communications monitoring can be an effective tool to detect and prevent terrorist and criminal attacks, helping to protect the safety and well-being of the population.

Strategic Intelligence: Monitoring electronic communications provides governments with valuable information about the intentions and capabilities of foreign actors, including hostile governments, terrorist organizations, and criminal groups. This strategic intelligence can help guide foreign policies, military operations, and national security decisions.

Here are some specific events that illustrate how strategic intelligence, supported by electronic communications monitoring, has influenced foreign policies, military operations and national security decisions:

- **The Cuban Missile Crisis (1962):** During the Cuban Missile Crisis, electronic communications monitoring was used by the United States to intercept and decrypt messages between Soviet and Cuban leaders. This intelligence provided crucial information about the Soviet Union's military plans and capabilities in Cuba, allowing the United States to make informed decisions and apply diplomatic pressure to resolve the crisis peacefully.

- **Operation Neptune Spear (2011):** Electronic communications monitoring played a crucial role in locating and tracking Osama bin Laden, leader of Al Qaeda, culminating in the US covert operation known as Neptune Spear. Intelligence obtained through electronic surveillance allowed American special forces to successfully carry out the raid on Abbottabad, Pakistan, where bin Laden was eventually found and eliminated.

- **The attack on the US Embassy in Benghazi**

(2012): After the attack on the US Embassy in Benghazi, Libya, electronic communications monitoring helped authorities track and capture those responsible for the attack. Intelligence obtained through electronic surveillance was instrumental in identifying perpetrators and coordinating law enforcement and counterterrorism operations.

These cases highlight how electronic communications monitoring has been used in critical situations to obtain strategic intelligence that has influenced political, military, and national security decisions.

Crime Solving: Analysis of electronic communications data can be useful in investigating and solving crimes, including serious crimes such as drug trafficking, human trafficking, and money laundering. Intelligence agencies can use this information to identify perpetrators, dismantle criminal networks, and conduct law enforcement operations.

The analysis of electronic communications data has been fundamental in numerous criminal investigations. Here are some examples:

- **The death of Jon Benét Ramsey:** In this high-profile 1996 case, analysis of emails and call logs was crucial in determining possible suspects and the connections between them. Although the case remains unsolved, analysis of electronic communications data remains an important tool for investigators working on it.

- **The murder of Hae Min Lee (Adnan Syed) - Serial Podcast:** Became the focus of the first season of the "Serial" podcast. Adnan Syed was convicted of the murder of his ex-girlfriend Hae Min Lee in 1999. Analysis of telephone call records and electronic communications data played a decisive role in the investigation and trial, providing clues to Syed 's movements and helping to build the prosecution case.

- **Operation Tandem (Spain):** In this police operation carried out in Spain in 2019, electronic communications data analysis was used to dismantle an international drug trafficking network. The authorities were able to track communications between members of the network, identify the main people involved and coordinate actions for their arrest and prosecution.

These examples illustrate how analyzing electronic communications data can provide valuable clues, establish connections between people and events, and significantly contribute to solving crimes.

The Beautiful

International collaboration: Electronic communications monitoring often involves collaboration between intelligence agencies of different countries, which can promote international cooperation in the fight against terrorism, organized crime and other transnational threats. This collaboration can help share information, resources, and best practices to address common security challenges.

There are several examples of cases in which international collaboration facilitated by the monitoring of electronic communications has been decisive in investigating and solving crimes, as well as in addressing threats to national security. Here are some examples:

- **Operation Emperor:** This operation was a joint effort by several law enforcement and intelligence agencies in Europe to dismantle a money laundering network linked to the Chinese mafia in 2012. Intelligence sharing and cooperation in monitoring electronic communications between countries such as Spain, France and Italy were fundamental to the success of the operation and the arrest of numerous suspects.

- **Terrorist attacks in Paris:** After the tragic terrorist attacks in Paris in November 2015, which left 130 dead, there was intense international collaboration between intelligence agencies of several countries. Information sharing through electronic communications monitoring helped identify perpetrators, their support networks, and prevent future planned attacks.

- **Case of the Argentine submarine ARA San Juan:** When the submarine disappeared in November 2017, an international search and rescue operation was unleashed. Collaboration between intelligence agencies from several countries made it possible to track electronic communications and geolocate possible signals from the submarine, which ultimately led to the discovery of its location and the clarification of the circumstances of its disappearance.

These cases highlight how international cooperation, facilitated by the exchange of information through the monitoring of electronic communications, can be vital in the fight against terrorism, organized crime and other challenges to national security. Collaboration between intelligence agencies from different countries makes it possible to take advantage of shared resources and knowledge to address common threats more effectively.

Technological innovation: The development and deployment of electronic communications monitoring technologies can drive advances in areas such as cryptography, artificial intelligence, and big data analysis. These innovations can have applications beyond national security, benefiting society at large in areas such as health, education, and the economy.

Here are some concrete examples of how technological innovation in electronic communications monitoring has benefited society in areas such as health, education and the economy:

- **Outbreak Detection:** In 2019, researchers used data from social media and electronic communications to track and predict outbreaks of mosquito-borne diseases in Brazil. The analysis of people's movement patterns made it possible to identify risk areas and take preventive measures to control the spread of diseases such as dengue and Zika.

- **Economic development:** In Singapore, the Government has used electronic communications data to analyze citizens' spending patterns and better understand their financial behaviors. This information is used to design economic policies that promote growth and sustainable development, as well as to identify investment opportunities in different sectors of the economy.

- **Prevention of financial fraud:** In the banking sector, electronic communications monitoring systems have been implemented to detect and prevent fraudulent activities, such as money laundering and credit card fraud. These systems use advanced algorithms to analyze large volumes of data and detect suspicious patterns of financial activity.

These examples illustrate how technological innovation in electronic communications monitoring can have a positive impact on society by improving public health, the economy, and financial security. However, it is important to ensure that the use of this technology is done ethically and respecting people's privacy and individual rights.

Accountability and oversight: In many democratic countries, monitoring of electronic communications is subject to judicial and parliamentary oversight, as well as accountability mechanisms. This helps ensure that the activities of intelligence agencies are within the legal framework and respect the civil rights and privacy of citizens. Here are some concrete examples:

- **United States Senate Intelligence Committee:** Oversees the activities of US intelligence agencies, including the National Security Agency (NSA). In 2013, after Edward Snowden revealed the extent of the NSA's electronic surveillance program, the committee conducted extensive investigations and public hearings to examine surveillance practices and ensure civil rights were respected.

- **UK Intelligence Oversight Act:** Establishes a legal framework for oversight of the activities of intelligence agencies, such as the Government Communication Headquarters (GCHQ). Under this law, the Intelligence Surveillance Commissioner was created, charged with reviewing the activities of the agencies and ensuring that they adhere to the law.

- **Australian Independent Review Committee Report:** Conducts regular reviews of the activities of Australian intelligence agencies. In its 2017 report, it recommended a series of changes to strengthen accountability and protect citizens' privacy.

- **Canadian Security and Privacy Review Commissioner:** Reviews the activities of intelligence agencies, such as the Canadian Communications Security Agency (CSE). In its 2019 report, the commissioner identified deficiencies in CSE oversight and recommended measures to improve the protection of citizens' privacy.

These are just a few examples of how accountability and oversight mechanisms are in action in different countries to ensure that monitoring of electronic communications is carried out within the legal framework and respecting the civil rights and privacy of citizens.

However, discretion and caution in the management of information in the field of intelligence are essential. As the 1974 "Rabin Report" suggests, publicly disclosing details about the operations of these agencies could compromise sources, agents, methods and operatives. Confidentiality stands as the cornerstone for the effectiveness of operations and to guarantee national security.

The Ugly

Privacy violation: Electronic communications monitoring may infringe citizens' rights to privacy and freedom of expression by collecting and analyzing their personal data without their consent. This raises ethical and legal concerns about the extent and nature of government surveillance in democratic societies. There are several examples of cases where privacy violations have occurred in the monitoring of electronic communications. Here are some examples:

- **The Edward Snowden Revelations (2013):** Edward Snowden, a former contractor for the United States National Security Agency (NSA), leaked classified documents that revealed mass surveillance programs carried out by the NSA and other intelligence agencies. These programs involved the indiscriminate collection of electronic communications data from U.S. citizens and foreigners, raising concerns about massive privacy violations.

- **The Cambridge Analytica Case (2018):** Political consulting firm Cambridge Analytica improperly obtained personal data from millions of Facebook users and used it to create psychographic profiles and target personalized political messages during the 2016 United States presidential election. This case highlights how the collection and misuse of electronic communications data can undermine people's privacy and manipulate democratic processes.

- **Team case (2015):** Exposed the activities of an Italian surveillance technology company. After being hacked, documents were leaked that revealed the sale of computer espionage tools to governments around the world.

These tools gave governments the ability to intercept electronic communications and access a wide range of information on electronic devices, including contacts, applications, calls, audio, camera, chat, passwords and more, thus compromising the privacy and security of users. citizens.

Two of the notable products of this company are Galileo and DaVinci, trade names of Remote-Control System. When the scandal was uncovered, it was revealed that countries such as Brazil, Chile, Colombia, Ecuador, Honduras, Mexico and Panama had acquired licenses to use these spy tools.

False positives and errors: Automated analysis of electronic communications data can generate false positives and errors, leading to unfair investigations, arbitrary detentions, and human rights violations. Additionally, mass data collection increases the risk of misidentification and misuse of sensitive information. Here I share some examples that serve to reflect on this delicate issue:

- **Name confusion:** In some cases, automated analysis systems may mistakenly identify people with names similar to known suspects. For example, a person with a common name could be incorrectly identified as a suspect in criminal activity due to an error in the analysis of communications data.

- **Message Misinterpretation:** Algorithms used to analyze text messages or online conversations may misinterpret the context or tone of conversations, leading to incorrect conclusions about the nature of communications. This can result in the misidentification of people as suspected of criminal or terrorist activities.

- **Detection of incorrect patterns:** Automated analysis systems can generate false positives by detecting patterns that are not related to criminal or terrorist activities. For example, an algorithm could mistakenly identify certain behaviors or keywords as indicators of suspicious activity, when in fact they are part of normal, legitimate activities.

Algorithms used in the analysis of electronic communications data can be biased by factors such as the quality of the training data or biases implicit in the algorithm design. This can lead to people being incorrectly identified as suspects based on characteristics such as race, religion, or political affiliation.

These examples illustrate how errors in the automated analysis of electronic communications data can generate false alarms and lead to unfair investigations or wrongful arrests. It is crucial to implement rigorous quality controls and oversight mechanisms to mitigate these risks and ensure accuracy and fairness in data analysis.

Finally, electronic communications monitoring in intelligence is a powerful tool that can provide valuable information for national security and crime prevention. **The good thing** lies in its ability to detect potential threats and protect society from imminent dangers. However, its implementation also raises ethical and legal challenges, as well as concerns about privacy and individual rights. **The beauty** of monitoring is its potential to strengthen the security and well-being of the population by identifying and neutralizing risks. On the other hand, **the ugly** manifests itself in the abuse of power and the violation of civil rights when it is used indiscriminately or without proper supervision and control. Ultimately, it is important to find a balance between the effectiveness of these practices and respect for democratic principles and fundamental human rights.

In summary, monitoring of electronic communications by intelligence agencies has positive aspects, such as threat prevention and international collaboration, but also poses significant challenges in terms of privacy, oversight, and risk of abuse of power. It is crucial to find a balance between national security and individual rights to guarantee a free and democratic society.

Metadata and Big Data: The challenge of data access and management

Metadata is like the digital fingerprints of our electronic communications. Although they do not contain the actual content of our messages, they reveal a surprising amount of information about who we are, what we do, and who we communicate with.

When we send an email or a text message, the content itself is comparable to the message written in a letter, while the metadata would be the information on the envelope: who sent it, who received it, the date, time and the location from which it is sent.

Why are these "digital envelopes" so important for national intelligence? To begin with, metadata can provide a complete picture of communication networks and relationships between individuals. For example, by analyzing metadata from phone calls, emails, or social media, intelligence agencies can identify patterns of behavior, connections between people, and even potential threats to national security.

Suppose you work as an intelligence analyst and you find the phone bill of someone who is being investigated in the neighborhood trash can. This bill includes the call report from the last cycle, where you discover indications that said person has been in frequent contact with individuals suspected of terrorist activities. This finding could alert you to the possibility that this individual is involved in illicit activities or is being recruited for terrorist activities. In this sense, metadata is an invaluable tool to prevent threats and protect the security of a country, without the need to invade people's privacy, since they do not provide access to the intimate content they have shared.

Additionally, they can help identify emerging trends, detect criminal or terrorist activity in real time, and provide crucial intelligence for national security decision-making. For example, analysis of social media metadata could reveal the spread of extremist propaganda or the coordination of terrorist attacks.

In other words, metadata is like small pieces of a puzzle that, when put together correctly, can provide a clear picture of the situation. In the context of national intelligence, they are an essential tool for understanding and addressing security threats, protecting citizens, and preserving the stability of a country.

The Great Dilemma: Metadata and personal privacy
The content of messages reveals intimate and personal details about people's conversations, opinions and emotions, while metadata provides more general information about communications without necessarily revealing the actual content of the messages. For this reason, **metadata analysis** is considered less invasive than **direct access to the content of electronic communications** due to the nature of the information they contain.

As I have already explained, metadata can include details such as who sends a message, who receives it, the time and duration of a phone call, the locations from which messages are sent, among others. While this information can be helpful in understanding people's connections and behavioral patterns, it does not reveal the exact content of what is being communicated. Therefore, although it partially affects privacy, it does not violate the privacy of communication. And that is important to understand.

In addition, metadata is considered part of the record of electronic communications that telecommunications companies and Internet service providers collect and store as part of their normal operations, in the telephone bill, in the yellow pages, affiliate club and any subscription service. This means that, in many cases, metadata is already being collected and stored by these companies for commercial purposes, such as efficient communications routing or billing for services.

However, it is important to note that although metadata may be less invasive compared to the content of communications, it can still reveal a significant amount of information about people's private lives and movements.

For this reason, access and use of metadata must also be subject to appropriate safeguards and controls to protect the civil rights and privacy of individuals.

State access to metadata in your daily life
In an increasingly digitalized world, where threats such as terrorism, organized crime and criminal activity are constantly evolving, allowing government agencies to access metadata is considered a necessary and indispensable measure to ensure a rapid and effective response. to possible risks to public safety.

Intelligence agencies are not interested in people's intimate private lives, and this is for three fundamental reasons: first, it is illegal to invade people's privacy; secondly, they do not have the resources to do so; and third, intimate content shared in communications is not necessary to achieve the goals of national security agencies.

Therefore, instead of reading text messages or emails, they are more interested in the general details: who is communicating with whom, when, and from where. These are metadata, seemingly insignificant pieces of information, but valuable because they can reveal crucial patterns and connections.

For example, a metadata analysis could detect a series of phone calls between suspicious individuals in a certain geographic area. This could alert authorities to possible criminal activity in progress and allow them to intervene quickly to prevent a serious incident. The Government needs metadata to manage, understand, enable access and preserve its vital assets over time and across domain uses.

In fact, State and Government access to metadata without the need for additional judicial authorization is based on a series of legal and national security considerations. In many countries, telecommunications, intelligence, and national security laws grant government agencies authority to collect and analyze metadata in the context of their national security and defense functions, preventing threats such as terrorism, organized crime, and criminal activity. However, this approach is not without controversy. It's a complex dilemma we face in the digital age, where security and privacy often conflict.

Importantly, access to metadata without additional judicial authorization also raises concerns about potential abuse of power and violation of individuals' civil rights and privacy. For this reason, it is essential that appropriate safeguards and controls are in place to ensure that access to metadata is used in a manner that is proportionate, transparent and subject to independent oversight.

Essential Controls: Protecting Access to Metadata

To ensure that access to metadata is used in a manner that is proportionate, transparent and subject to independent oversight, it is essential to implement a series of appropriate safeguards and controls. Some important measures could include:

- **Judicial Oversight:** Establish a system in which a judge

authorizes and oversees access to metadata, ensuring that it is adequately justified and limited to legitimate cases related to national security or the prevention of serious crime.
- **Legal restrictions:** Define clear and precise limits for access to metadata through specific laws, specifying the legitimate purposes for which it can be used and the circumstances under which its collection and analysis is permitted.
- **Transparency:** Ensure that policies and practices related to access to metadata are transparent and accessible to the public, allowing citizens to understand how and why their data is used in this way.
- **Independent oversight:** Create independent oversight mechanisms, such as privacy commissions or data protection agencies, charged with monitoring and evaluating compliance with laws and policies related to access to metadata.
- **Data Minimization:** Apply data minimization principles to limit the collection and retention of metadata to only what is strictly necessary to fulfill legitimate purposes established by law.
- **Human rights protection:** Ensure that access to metadata respects fundamental human rights, such as the right to privacy and freedom of expression, avoiding any form of discrimination or unfair profiling.
- **Accountability:** Identify effective accountability mechanisms to hold government agencies and officials responsible for access to metadata accountable in the event of abuse or misuse of this information.

Implementing these measures can help balance the legitimate need to access metadata with the protection of individual rights and citizen privacy. At the end of the day, a balance needs to be found between protecting public safety and respecting individual rights. It is a conversation that we must all participate in, as it directly affects our society and our daily lives.

Books / movies and series - 60 key facts

[Intelligence, Transparency and Accountability]

BOOKS:

1. *"Failure of Intelligence: The Decline and Fall of the CIA"* – Melvin A. Goodman, 2008

The author argues for a delicate balance between national security and oversight, while recognizing the importance of congressional oversight to ensure CIA accountability, warning of the risks of excessive oversight that could hamper intelligence operations. Therefore, it highlights the need for effective communication and collaboration between the CIA and oversight committees to maintain such balance.

The book advocates for deep soul-searching about the role of the CIA and the intelligence community at large, especially in light of recent failures related to the collapse of the Soviet Union, the September 11, 2001 attacks, and the Iraq war. Goodman argues that the CIA, despite its large budget, has proven unable to provide reliable strategic warnings and, worse still, has manipulated intelligence information for political purposes. It proposes that reform of the intelligence enterprise will only be possible when the link between intelligence and politics is understood and debated, advocating for an intelligence agency free of political influences.

In this crucial and timely book, the author provocatively combines history with contemporary political analysis and reform proposals that challenge conventional perceptions about clandestine intelligence collection. Goodman persuasively argues that the lack of diplomatic relations has contributed to the inability to collect effective intelligence, thus highlighting the urgent need to rethink and reform national intelligence management. Available in English at this link: https://amzn.to/3PYbNig

2. *"Accountability and the law"* - Transparency and Accountability versus Secrecy in Intelligence Operations | Arianna Vedaschi, 2021

This text reviews the Italian intelligence system from a public law perspective, highlighting the tension between transparency and accountability in these operations. The book delves into the complex search for a balance between the need for secrecy for reasons of national security and the importance of transparency and public accountability.

Through detailed analysis, historical cases are explored that exemplify the challenges and implications of this balance in intelligence activities. The various facets of the debate are carefully examined, considering how the policies of transparency and accountability can coexist with the legitimate demands of national security and the protection of sensitive information.

Ultimately, the work offers valuable reflection on how to find an appropriate balance between these principles in the context of intelligence operations, highlighting the importance of law and legal mechanisms to ensure that the power of intelligence is subject to the democratic controls and public accountability. It can be consulted and downloaded completely free of charge at the following link: https://doi.org/10.4324/9781003168331

3. *"Intelligence and Surprise Attack: Failure and Success from Pearl Harbor to 9/11 and Beyond"* - Erik J. Dahl, 2013

In "Intelligence and Surprise Attacks: Failure and Success from Pearl Harbor to 9/11 and Beyond" by Erik J. Dahl, published in 2013, the author challenges the conventional notion of intelligence failure in surprise attacks. Contrary to the common belief that attacks succeed because important warnings are lost in the noise or a lack of imagination and collaboration among intelligence officials to "connect the dots" of available information, Dahl proposes a different perspective.

Dahl's central argument is that success is not based on greater imagination or analysis, but on an improvement in the acquisition of intelligence at the tactical level and in the willingness of leaders to listen and act on the warnings of their personnel. intelligence. Rather than focusing on the ability to "connect the dots", Dahl highlights the importance of having responsive and proactive leaders who are willing to make informed decisions based on the intelligence received.

In summary, the book offers an innovative perspective on the role of intelligence in preventing surprise attacks, underscoring the importance of effective intelligence acquisition and responsive leadership as crucial elements for success in detecting and preventing threats. Its English version is available on Amazon https://amzn.to/3THSxGP

4. *"The Code Book: The Secret History of Codes and Codebreaking"* -Simon Singh, 1999

This wonderful work immerses the reader in the fascinating search for secrets hidden in codes, from Egyptian enigmas to the sophisticated computer encryptions of the modern era.

Singh presents a captivating narrative that covers the evolution of cryptography throughout history, from the primitive cipher systems used in ancient times to the cutting-edge encryption methods used in today's digital world. The author explores various aspects related to cryptography, from its crucial role in war and diplomacy to the mathematical advances that have driven the development of increasingly complex encryption systems.

Additionally, the book addresses the ethical and legal challenges that arise in the digital age regarding privacy and security, offering a considered and insightful perspective on these hot-button issues. With an interdisciplinary approach that interweaves history, science and technology, "The Secret Code" provides a complete and captivating vision of the exciting world of secret codes and cryptography. Available to purchase on Amazon in English only at https://amzn.to/3VCOsWP_but also, it can be consulted totally free in Spanish (only for academic purposes) at the following link: The secret codes - Simon Singh (librosmaravillosos.com)

5. *"God's Spy"* - Juan Gómez-Jurado, 2022

"God's Spy" by Juan Gómez-Jurado is an exciting thriller that immerses us in the secrets of the Vatican and the Eternal City. Set in Rome after the death of Pope John Paul II, the plot follows Inspector Paola Dicanti as she investigates the murder of two influential cardinals, revealing dark secrets and conspiracies in the upper echelons of the Church.

In the midst of preparations for the papal conclave, Dicanti faces a serial killer whose crimes are marked by a macabre ritual and messages encrypted with religious symbols. As she digs deeper into the investigation, she discovers the existence of a rehabilitation center for priests with a history of sexual abuse, unearthing more secrets that challenge faith and morality.

The novel offers valuable lessons for intelligence agencies, highlighting the importance of transparency, accountability and collaboration between different agencies to confront complex challenges. In a world where the truth can be as elusive as it is deadly, "God's Spy" raises the need for cunning, cooperation and caution in the search for the truth. You can get it on Amazon at this link: https://amzn.to/3Ua0NRg

6. **"Eight suspects, one culprit"** - Actus Deouf, 2023

The book collection "Eight suspects, one culprit" offers an exciting experience with Alex, a perceptive detective willing to solve the most intriguing cases. Throughout six separate investigations, readers are immersed in a series of puzzles and challenges, from deciphering secret codes to analyzing testimonies, all with the goal of identifying the culprit among the suspects. Each case features a variety of games and puzzles, such as scrambled words, anagrams and sudoku, that not only entertain but also stimulate critical thinking and problem solving.

This publication not only provides entertainment, but also encourages the development of important skills for young readers. By facing the challenges posed in each investigation, they have the opportunity to improve their analytical skills, attention to detail, and problem-solving skills. Additionally, the book includes an accompanying guide for parents in the prologue, offering valuable advice to support children during their detective adventure and get the most out of each case.

With its combination of mystery, challenge and skill development, "8 Suspects, One Guilty" promises to provide an exciting and educational experience. Through this book, readers can embark on intriguing adventures while cultivating valuable skills that will serve them in their daily lives and personal development. It is available on Amazon Spanish and in English, here is the link to the Spanish version https://amzn.to/3J9TDGj

FILMS:

1. **"Erin Brockovich"** – (USA, 2000)

[Accountability]

The film "Erin Brockovich ", starring Julia Roberts, tells the true story of a single mother who challenges a powerful energy company in a fight for justice that culminates in a historic $333 million settlement for affected victims. Although it is not a spy film, it offers an interesting look at tenacity, exhaustive research, empathy with those affected, adherence to ethical values and social responsibility. These lessons can be applied by intelligence agencies in their search for truth and justice, showing how a determined person can make a difference and meet challenges head-on.

2. **"The lives of others"** – (Germany, 2006)

[Privacy violation]

Ranked #6 among the best German films of all time, this multi-award-winning drama starring Ulrich Mühe and Sebastian Koch offers a moving and thoughtful perspective on state surveillance, political oppression, and the transformative power of art under a regime. totalitarian. The plot raises important ethical questions about privacy and the human impact of espionage, showing how mistrust can affect personal and professional relationships. In addition, it provokes reflections on professional ethics in intelligence work and the human capacity for change, highlighting the importance of balancing security with respect for civil rights. These lessons are relevant both in the historical context of East Germany and in the modern field of intelligence, where the protection of privacy and respect for individual rights are crucial issues.

3. **"A call to spy"** – (USA, 2019)

[Recruitment innovation]

With the original title A Call to Spy, is a drama based on true events starring Sarah Megan Thomas, Stana Katic and Radhika Apte and focuses on the early days of World War II, when Winston Churchill orders the creation of a spy agency to recruit and train female spies. The film highlights the importance of innovation in recruiting, adaptability and creativity in the field of espionage, as well as the courage and sacrifice of agents. Additionally, it highlights the consequences of covert operations and the importance of local resistance and support for the success of intelligence missions. Although the film has its critics, it offers an interesting look at the spy genre from a different angle and highlights the bravery and determination of these women in times of conflict.

4. **"La infiltrada"** - The Operative (FRA, 2019)

[Control judicial]

Also known as "The Operative", this psychological thriller is based on the Hebrew novel "The English Teacher" (המורה לאנגלית) written by Yiftach Reicher- Atir, a former intelligence officer. The story follows Rachel, a young woman recruited by the Mossad to infiltrate Tehran, facing moral dilemmas and emotional challenges while working as an undercover agent. This intriguing thriller explores themes of identity, betrayal and loyalty in the world of international espionage, offering constant suspense and unexpected twists. Additionally, it shows how personal relationships can complicate undercover operations and the importance of judicial oversight to ensure that officers' actions remain within legal limits.

5. **"Spy: A clueless spy"** – Spy | spy (USA, 2015)

[Team humor and morale]

"Spy", starring Melissa McCarthy and Jason Statham, is an action comedy about Susan Cooper, a CIA analyst who volunteers for a covert mission. Although initially undervalued, Susan demonstrates her intelligence and bravery as she faces off against enemies and immerses herself in the world of espionage. The film calls not to underestimate any agent, highlights the importance of adaptability and continuous training, the use of technology in espionage, teamwork and communication, as well as the role of humor in improving morale. and team efficiency.

SERIES:

1. **"Eye in the Sky"** – (HKG, 2015)

[20 Episodes | 1 Season]

"Eye in the Sky" is a Hong Kong television series that focuses on the operations of the Department of National Intelligence and addresses issues related to state surveillance, transparency and accountability in intelligence. Throughout the series, a group of intelligence agents as they carry out covert missions to protect national security and confront various threats. The ethical and moral complexities of state surveillance are explored, as well as the implications of the lack of transparency and accountability in surveillance activities. intelligence. Available on Curiositystream and other platforms

On the other hand, the movie "Eye in the Sky", directed by Gavin Hood and released in 2015, is a British-American suspense thriller that focuses on a covert operation to capture terrorists in Kenya. Although both works share the title "Eye in the Sky" and deal with intelligence and security issues, differ in their focus, plot and context. The TV series focuses on espionage and intelligence operations in Hong Kong, while the film focuses on an international counterterrorism operation in Africa. Available on Apple TV.

2. **"Rubicon"** (USA, 2010)

[13 Episodes | 1 Season]

"Rubicon" is a series inspired by the political thrillers of the 1970s, set in a New York-based government intelligence agency, where nothing is as it seems. Will Travers, a brilliant man with an aptitude for pattern recognition, is the leader of a team of analysts at American Policy Institute in

New York City, faces tragedy and discovers hidden clues in communications that could lead to a complex and sinister conspiracy with devastating implications for national security.

The series addresses topics such as state surveillance, transparency and accountability in intelligence, as it explores the ethical and moral complexities of the world of intelligence and espionage. Depending on your region, you could get it on AMC+, Prime Video and Sling TV, Apple TV or Google Play Store, among other platforms.

3. **"Condor"** (USA, 2018)

[20 Episodes | 2 Seasons]

"Condor" is based on the novel "Six Days of the Condor" by James Grady and inspired by the film " Three days of the Condor" from 1975. The plot follows Joe Turner, a young CIA analyst who becomes involved in a massive conspiracy after his team is murdered. As he tries to uncover the truth, he finds himself caught up in a dangerous web of intrigue, deception, and betrayal involving top government officials and powerful corporations. Discovering that the CIA has been using an algorithm he developed to spy on American citizens.

Joe Turner's fight for truth and justice calls into question the morality of covert operations and the need for transparency in government. The series shows how intelligence agencies can operate in the shadows and carry out activities that challenge democratic principles. Although inspired by a classic film, it offers a contemporary perspective on intelligence and the struggle to balance national security and individual rights. You can see it on Prime Video, MGM Plus, and other platforms, depending on your region.

4. **"Alex Rider"** (UK, 2020)

[24 Episodes | 3 Seasons]

"Alex Rider" is based on the popular book series of the same name written by Anthony Horowitz. The story follows Alex, an orphaned teenager who finds himself unexpectedly involved in the world of espionage after discovering that his only uncle, apparently killed in an accident, was an MI6 spy. The organization recruits Alex to carry out undercover missions as he investigates the mysterious death of his uncle and faces various threats and conspiracies.

Although the series focuses on action and espionage, it also explores deeper themes such as state surveillance, transparency and accountability in the field of intelligence. As Alex assumes his role as a spy, he is confronted with ethical dilemmas and questions the legitimacy of secret operations and the lack of accountability. In dangerous situations, Alex must make difficult decisions that affect both the public welfare and his personal duty. You can enjoy it on Prime Video, Movistar Plus and other streaming platforms.

5. **"Totally Spies!"** - KC Special Agent (FRA-CAN, 2001)
[156 Episodes | 6 Seasons]

" Totally Spies !" is a French-Canadian animated series, starring three teenage girls: Sam, Clover and Alex, who have been trained as undercover agents for an international spy organization. They lead seemingly normal lives as high school students, but are always ready to Confront villains and stop threats that endanger global security.

Aimed primarily at a youth audience, the series combines elements of comedy, action and adventure. Each episode presents new missions and challenges for the protagonists. Get ready to enjoy the exciting adventures of these teenage spies! Available on Prime Video and other paid streaming platforms, also, on Serieslan.com you can watch it for free in Latin Spanish.

In the complex field of intelligence, where state security agencies possess considerable power to influence both national and international affairs, transparency and accountability become fundamental requirements. These principles are essential to maintain a balance between national security and respect for individual rights in a democratic society.

Operating with transparency means communicating methods and operations within limits that do not compromise national security. Furthermore, it is crucial that agencies justify their actions and take responsibility for any consequences arising from them.

Electronic communications monitoring plays a crucial role in protecting national security and the well-being of citizens, despite the privacy concerns it may raise. From threat prevention to international collaboration, this practice has been valuable in the fight against terrorism and organized crime.

Access to metadata raises ethical and privacy challenges, but also offers opportunities to protect public safety. However, it is essential to implement adequate controls to guarantee its proportional and transparent use, thus protecting the individual rights of citizens.

The conversation about transparency, accountability and access to data is crucial and must involve everyone. It is essential to continue reflecting on these issues and seek a balance that protects both national security and the individual rights of citizens.

Remember that you can delve deeper into these topics by watching the movies and series that I have placed in this chapter. After watching them, if you feel like sharing your thoughts or discussing this topic further, I would be happy to hear from you. Your opinions and reflections are valuable and can enrich this conversation about a safer and more ethical digital future.

Let me know, what do you think about the State's access to metadata without additional judicial authorization? Do you think it is a necessary measure to guarantee public safety or do you consider it to be an unjustified intrusion into people's privacy? You can do so in the review of this book on Amazon, on my website www.mujersegura.com or by sending me a message on the main social networks with the user @mujerseguridad. I look forward to hearing your point of view!

CHAPTER 6: INTELLIGENCE IS IN FASHION

In the information age, data analysis talent has become one of the most sought-after skills. This chapter is dedicated to those who see in numbers something more than figures, stories, predictions and solutions.

Opportunities for people with talent in data analysis

Today's world is full of data waiting to be interpreted. Organizations tirelessly seek professionals capable of turning this data into intelligent strategies and decisions. If you have the ability to decipher the language of data, countless doors are ready to open before you.

Boost your career with online training resources, education has never been so accessible like now. With an abundance of online training resources, you can boost your career from anywhere in the world.

In this chapter I will guide you through the best platforms and tools that will help you hone your analytical and technological skills.

Unlock your future with scholarships and facilities, education is an investment in your future, and scholarships and financial facilities can be the springboard you need. We will explore how to take advantage of these opportunities to advance your education without financial obstacles limiting your potential.

It doesn't matter if you are a police officer, civilian, military, your sex, age, origin, language, religion, or any other characteristic, this career has a universe of opportunities and possibilities. Are you ready to immerse yourself in this fascinating journey towards learning and personal growth? Join me as we explore the infinite possibilities that the digital universe has to offer you. It's time to become the secret agent of your own destiny and unleash your full potential in the exciting field of technology and data.

In the following pages, I will need all your attention possible. Get ready to unlock your future and exploit your potential with data and technology. This chapter is more than a read; is a map to your success in the dynamic field of data analysis. Start your journey today!

Develop your talent: Opportunities in data analysis
Discover how to develop your skills in social media data analysis to make the most of the job opportunities available. From identifying emerging trends to understanding user behavior, social media data analysis is an essential skill in today's world of work.

Online courses: Explore various social media data analytics training options through platforms such as Coursera, Udemy, and LinkedIn Learning. Some courses featured include:
- Social Media Analytics: Using Data to Understand Public Conversations (Coursera)
- Applied Social Network Analysis in Python (Coursera)
- Data Science for Social Scientists (Coursera)
- Social Media Marketing Specialization (Coursera)
- Mining Social Media Data in R (DataCamp)
- Social Media Strategy for Small Businesses (LinkedIn Learning)
- Introduction to Social Media Investigation: A Hands-

on Approach (Udemy)
- Social Media Analytics: Hands-on (Udemy)
- Advanced Social Media Strategy for Public Relations (Udemy)
- Intelligence Analysis in the Age of Big Data (edX)

These courses offer a variety of approaches, from fundamentals to advanced techniques, for social media data analysis and open-source intelligence.

To access online courses, follow these steps:
1. **Select a platform:** Choose from popular platforms such as Coursera, Udemy, LinkedIn Learning, edX, and DataCamp.
2. **Find the course:** Use the search function to find the course that interests you, either by title, topic, or related keywords.
3. **Review the description:** Make sure the course meets your expectations by reviewing details such as content, duration, and prerequisites.
4. **Check availability:** Confirm that the course is available in your language and region.
5. **Sign up:** Follow the instructions to sign up, creating an account if necessary.

As for the cost, this can vary depending on the platform, the duration and quality of the content, as well as the reputation of the instructor. Some platforms offer free courses, while others require a one-time payment or a monthly subscription. Check the pricing details on each course page and keep an eye out for discounts or promotions.

Specialized Certifications: Explore specialized certifications in social media data analysis and open-source intelligence, which may be offered by various academic institutions or training organizations, such as:
- Certification in Social Data Analysis (SDA)

- Certificate in Open-Source Intelligence (OSINT)
- Certification in Social Network Data Analysis (SNDA)
- Certificate in Digital Research and Social Network Analysis
- Certified Social Media Intelligence Professional (CSMIP)

To apply for certifications specialized in social media data analysis and open-source intelligence, you generally must follow these steps:

1. **Research:** Research the different certifications available in social media data analysis and open-source intelligence. Look for recognized and well-rated programs in the field.
2. **Admission requirements:** Read the admission requirements of each certification carefully. This may include criteria such as educational level, previous work experience, specific skills, and prior knowledge on the subject.
3. **Preparation:** Prepare to meet the admission requirements. If necessary, acquire the required skills and knowledge through online courses, tutorials, books or relevant work experience.
4. **Registration:** Once you are ready, proceed to register for certification. This may involve completing an online application form, providing relevant documentation and paying a registration fee.
5. **Exam or Assessment:** Some certifications may require you to pass an exam or participate in an assessment to demonstrate your skills and knowledge in the field. Prepare properly for these tests.
6. **Stay up to date:** Once you become certified, it is important to stay up to date with the latest trends and advancements in the field. Participate in continuing professional development activities and continue learning new skills.

7. **Practical application:** Use your new skills and knowledge in social media data analysis and open-source intelligence in your work or personal projects. This will help you consolidate what you have learned and demonstrate the value of your certification in real situations.

Remember that each certification may have its own specific procedures and requirements, so it is important to follow the instructions provided by the entity that grants the certification.

Graduate Programs: Universities around the world offer graduate programs in data analytics, data science, artificial intelligence, and related fields. Some examples are:
- **Master in Data Science** - University of Buenos Aires (Argentina)
- Master in Data Science and Information Engineering - University of Chile (Chile)
- **Master in Data Science** - University of Barcelona (Spain)
- **Master in Artificial Intelligence** - Polytechnic University of Catalonia (Spain)
- **Master in Data Analysis for Science and Business** - Autonomous University of Madrid (Spain)
- **Master in Data Science and Big Data** - Carlos III University of Madrid (Spain)
- **Master in Data Science and Business Analytics** - Polytechnic University of Valencia (Spain)
- **Master in Artificial Intelligence and Deep Learning** - University Pierre and Marie Curie (Spain)
- **Master in Data Analysis and Big Data** - University of Salamanca (Spain)
- **Master in Machine Learning and Data Science** – University Pompeu Fabra (Spain)
- **Master in Artificial Intelligence and Intelligent Systems** - Polytechnic University of Madrid (Spain)

- **Master in Data Sciences and Artificial Intelligence** - University College Dublin (United States)
- **Master in Data Science and Analytics Business** - Carnegie Mellon University (United States)
- **Master in Applied Data Science** - University of Michigan (United States)
- **Master in Artificial Intelligence and Intelligent Systems** - Université Pierre et Marie Curie (France)
- **Master in Data Science and Machine Learning** - Imperial College London (United Kingdom)

Please remember that this list is just a sample of the many programs available around the world and that each may have specific admission requirements, curricular focuses, and program length. I recommend you research in detail about those that interest you to find the one that best suits your needs and professional objectives. Make sure you meet the requirements and prepare a strong application that highlights your achievements and contributions in the field of study. Success in this adventure!

University Degree available in the Dominican Republic:
The educational landscape in the Dominican Republic offers a wide range of undergraduate and graduate programs in areas such as information technology, cybersecurity, defense and national security, as well as data science.

Among these programs, options stand out such as the Master's Degree in Information and Communication Technology Management offered by the Pontificia Universidad Católica Madre y Maestra (PUCMM), which, although it does not focus exclusively on the analysis of data in social networks, addresses issues relevant in the management of information and communications technology, including computer security.

Similarly, the Master in Data Science at the Universidad Iberoamericana (UNIBE) offers a diverse approach in data science that may include social media data analysis depending on specific courses and approaches. On the other hand, the Master's Degree in Information Security at the Autonomous University of Santo Domingo (UASD) focuses on crucial aspects of information security, such as data protection and open-source intelligence in the field of cybersecurity.

In addition, institutions such as the University of the Caribbean (UNICARIBE), the Technological Institute of Santo Domingo (INTEC), and the National University for Defense (UNADE), among others, also offer relevant undergraduate and graduate programs in areas such as cybersecurity, analysis of data and information technology, providing diverse options for those interested in these emerging fields.

I suggest you review the specific details of each program, such as admission requirements, pedagogical approaches, application deadlines, and associated costs. You can do this by visiting the websites of the mentioned institutions or by contacting them directly. It is important to carefully review the admission requirements and prepare the necessary documents, such as academic transcripts and letters of recommendation, as requested by each university.

Remember that these examples are only a sample of the programs available. The educational field in these areas is constantly changing, with the opening of new programs. I encourage you to regularly explore the portals of these universities and other educational institutions to be aware of new opportunities.

Boost your career with online training resources

Attending seminars, workshops and conferences specialized in social media data analysis is a great way to gain knowledge and skills in this constantly evolving field. These events are hosted by a variety of academic institutions, technology companies, and professional organizations, and offer valuable opportunities to learn about the latest trends, research, and practical applications.

Academic institutions: Universities and research centers often organize seminars and workshops as part of their academic programs or specialized events. These events are designed for both students and professionals interested in delving into data analysis on social networks.

Seminar "Current Trends in Data Analysis in Social Networks" - Stanford University: Explore the latest trends in data analysis in social networks, covering topics such as analysis techniques and emerging tools.

Workshop "Practical Applications of Open-Source Intelligence in National Security" - International Cyber Security Institute (IISC): Provides practical examples on the use of open-source intelligence in national security.

Seminar "Ethics in the Analysis of Social and Open-Source Data" - Harvard University Center for Digital Ethics: Examines the ethical dilemmas associated with the collection and use of data on social networks and open sources.

Workshop "Advanced Tools for Social Network Analysis" - Association of Social Data Analysts (SADA): Presents advanced tools and techniques for social network analysis, with a focus on practical applications.

Seminar "Challenges and Opportunities in Open-Source Intelligence for Criminal Investigation" - National Criminal Intelligence Center (CENIC): Analyzes the specific challenges and opportunities related to open-source intelligence in the context of criminal investigation.

Seminar "Data Analysis Workshop on Social Networks" - Autonomous University of Santo Domingo (UASD): Shows specific data analysis techniques for social networks, including data collection, cleaning, analysis and visualization.

Technology companies - Large technology companies, especially those that offer tools and platforms for social media data analysis, often organize events as part of their training and professional development programs.

Seminar "Advanced Tools for Data Extraction and Analysis in Social Networks" - International Association of Intelligence Analysts (IAA): Explore advanced tools and techniques for data analysis in social networks.

Workshop "Practical Applications of Python and R in Data Analysis in Social Networks" - DataCamp: Offers practical examples on the use of Python and R for data analysis in social networks.

Seminar "Introduction to Text Mining and Sentiment Analysis in Social Networks" - Columbia University: Offers an introduction to text mining and sentiment analysis techniques applied to data in social networks.

Workshop "Using Data Visualization Tools in Social Networks to Identify Patterns" - LinkedIn Learning: Teaches how to use data visualization tools to identify patterns and trends in social network data.

Learning Applications in Data Analysis in Social Networks" - Massachusetts Institute of Technology (MIT): Explore various *machine learning* applications in data analysis in social networks, from classification to generation of recommendations.
Specialist conferences and events: In addition to seminars and workshops, there are a variety of specialist data analytics and social media conferences and events held regularly around the world. These events attract a wide range of professionals and academics and offer opportunities to learn about the latest trends, research and practical applications in the field.

Strata Data Conference: Hosted by O'Reilly Media, this conference focuses on big data, *machine learning*, and data analytics. Includes sessions on data analysis on social networks and other open sources.

IEEE International Conference on Data Mining (ICDM): This event is one of the leading academic conferences in the field of data mining. Includes topics related to data analysis in social networks and open sources.

ACM SIGKDD Conference on Knowledge Discovery and Data Mining (KDD): Known as KDD, this conference is one of the most important in the field of data science and knowledge discovery. Presents research on data analysis on social networks and other open sources.

International AAAI Conference on Web and Social Media (ICWSM): This conference focuses on research on online social networks and web platforms. Includes sessions on data analysis in social networks and text mining.

Open-Source Intelligence Summit: Hosted by the International Cyber Security Institute (IISC), this event focuses on open-source intelligence and cybersecurity. Presents case studies and advanced data analysis techniques.

International Conference on Social Media & Society (SMSociety): This conference brings together researchers and professionals interested in the social impact of social media. Includes sessions on data analysis in social networks and research ethics.

Global Investigative Journalism Conference: Although not focused exclusively on data analysis, this event brings together investigative journalists from around the world and often includes sessions on the use of open data in investigative journalism.

These are just a few examples of conferences and events specializing in data analytics and open-source intelligence that take place regularly around the world. Each of these events offers unique opportunities to learn about the latest trends, share knowledge, and establish professional networks in the field. I would recommend doing more research on each event to determine which one best suits your specific interests and needs.

Internal learning: Many organizations and companies offer internal training programs in social media data analysis for their employees. These programs may include training sessions, mentoring, and hands-on learning opportunities on real projects.

Regardless of which option you choose, it is important to look for training programs that are up to date with the latest trends and technologies in social media data analysis, and that provide you with the skills and knowledge necessary to succeed in this ever-evolving field.

Internal training programs that enhance your professional profile

Data analysis: These usually address topics such as data collection, cleaning, analysis and visualization. They may include courses on statistics, data mining, machine learning, and specific data analysis tools.

Cybersecurity: They cover aspects such as the protection of computer systems, threat detection, security incident management and information security. They may also include training in ethical hacking techniques and cyberattack prevention.

Open-Source Intelligence (OSINT): They focus on the collection and analysis of information from open sources, such as social networks, public websites, and online databases. Courses may include advanced search techniques, social network analysis, and source credibility assessment.

National security and defense: They are designed for civil, military and police professionals who work or aspire to work in areas related to national security and defense. They may cover topics such as strategic intelligence, cybersecurity, counterintelligence, and crisis management.

Data management: They focus on the effective management of data within an organization. They include topics such as databases, data warehousing, data governance, and regulatory compliance.

Predictive analytics: Teach how to use historical data to predict future trends and make informed decisions. They include predictive modeling techniques, time series analysis and optimization.

Internal training programs in data analytics, cybersecurity, open-source intelligence, and related areas are vital to keeping staff up-to-date and improving their skills in increasingly critical fields in today's environment. These programs are typically offered by governments, intelligence agencies, government organizations, private companies, and universities. They can vary in length and format, from short courses and workshops to certificate and graduate programs.

If you are part of any of these entities, you have a good chance of qualifying. Research with your colleagues and related people. Take advantage of all the opportunities!

Unlock your future with scholarships and facilities

In an increasingly digitalized and connected environment, intelligence agencies play a vital role in the protection and security of nations. In this context, access to technology and security training becomes an invaluable asset for those who aspire to contribute to the field of intelligence and national security. Discover how these technology and security scholarships can open doors for you in a constantly evolving field, and how you can make the most of these opportunities to advance your career and contribute to the world of intelligence.

Scholarships and opportunities by country: Governments in many countries offer scholarships and funding programs for studies in high-demand areas, such as information technology and cybersecurity. Visit the websites of the ministries of education or relevant government agencies in your country for information on available scholarships. As an example, here are some:

Australia: Australia Awards Scholarship Programme.
Brazil: Science Program without Borders.
Canada: Emerging Leaders in the Americas Program (ELAP).
China: Chinese Government Scholarship (CSC) and Ministry of Education (MOE) International Student Scholarship Program.
Spain: Carolina Foundation and MAEC-AECID Scholarship Program.
USA: Fulbright Program and International Student Scholarship Program (ISB).
India: University Grants Council of India (UGC).
Israel: Israel Government Scholarship and MASHAV Scholarship.
Japan: Government of Japan Scholarship Program (Monbukagakusho).

Scholarships in Dominican Republic:
Ministry of Higher Education, Science and Technology (MESCYT): Manages and awards national and international scholarships for undergraduate and graduate programs in various areas and modalities, including information technology and cybersecurity. Visit the official MESCYT website for updated information on available scholarships. Every year, thousands of people can apply online and benefit from pursuing the academic program of their dreams. And if you come from the UASD, as was my case, the financial allowance for maintenance abroad is higher. They also have special scholarships for women and other interest groups. Find out. Take advantage of all the advantages!

Scholarships and Opportunities by Organization: It is common for international organizations to promote scholarship programs and training opportunities in fields related to cybersecurity, telecommunications and intelligence, because they have many agencies that address these issues and frequently require trained personnel in those areas. areas. It's time to explore! Here are some examples:

Organization of American States (OAS): Promotes postgraduate scholarships and training courses in information technology and cybersecurity, telecommunications, intelligence and gender equality in technology, among them the "OAS Intelligence" stands out. Studies Scholarship Program", together with the "OAS Telecommunications Scholarships", the "OAS Cyberwomen Scholarship Program" and the "OAS Cybersecurity Professional Development Scholarships" that sponsors specialized training, workshops and conferences at educational institutions associated with the OAS.

United Nations Organization (UN): Through the United Nations Fellowships Program there are scholarships available from short-term courses to specialized training, in addition to those offered by its specialized agencies and other emblematic programs, such as the ITU Scholarship Programme, the UN Cybersecurity Training Programme, the UN Cyberwoman, and the UN Intelligence and Security Training Programme.

European Union: Programs such as Erasmus Mundus, Marie Skłodowska -Curie Actions (MSCA), EU Cybersecurity Program, EU Women4Cyber Initiative have allowed the EU to finance scholarships, projects and activities related to research for improvements in cybersecurity, telecommunications and intelligence.

Private organizations and foundations: Beyond governments, there is a vast world of opportunities waiting to be discovered in private organizations, companies and foundations committed to educational development. From scholarships to funding in fields as diverse as technology, cybersecurity, STEM and more, there are a range of possibilities that will surprise you.

Carlos Slim Foundation: This foundation is a beacon of support for students and professionals, providing scholarships and programs designed to boost talent in essential areas such as computing, software engineering, and cybersecurity.

Fulbright Foundation: If you are a US or international citizen, this foundation offers you a wide range of opportunities, including scholarships in such vital fields as information technology and computing.

Rockefeller Foundation: Dive into the vast ocean of possibilities offered by the Rockefeller Foundation, with scholarships and grants aimed at projects that address social and environmental challenges, including the intersection between technology and society.

Soros Foundation: With a global reach, the Soros Foundation supports students around the world, including in crucial areas such as information technology and cybersecurity. Get ready to discover exciting and transformative opportunities.

Google: Are you passionate about information technology? Google offers you a world of possibilities through scholarships and support programs designed for students and professionals in related fields. It's your chance to take the next step in your career.

Microsoft: From technological innovation to the empowerment of minorities and underrepresented groups, Microsoft is committed to the future of information technology and computer science. Discover their scholarship and support programs, your path to success could start here!

Remember that this list is just a sample of the many opportunities available, check their official portals regularly, as new opportunities may arise. Additionally, be sure to meet the specific requirements of each scholarship and prepare a strong application that highlights your skills and achievements in the field of study.

Universities and research centers websites: Many universities and research centers offer specific programs designed to benefit women and other minority groups as part of inclusion and diversity initiatives in the field of technology, cybersecurity, intelligence and related areas. Here are some ways to find information about these scholarship programs:

Online Scholarship Platforms: There are several online platforms that collect information on scholarships in different areas of study. Some of the most popular include:

1. **Scholarship Portal:** This platform offers an extensive database of international scholarships in various fields, including information technology and cybersecurity.
2. **Scholarships.com:** Another platform that provides information about scholarships in a variety of areas, including technology and communication.
3. **Fastweb:** It is a platform that offers resources on scholarships, financial aid and internships, including opportunities in fields related to technology and computing.

Visit the websites of universities, colleges and specialized organizations. Join online professional networks and communities. Attend events and conferences, this way you will increase your network of contacts.

If you dare to challenge the limits and explore your full potential in the fascinating world of data and technology, don't wait any longer to act! While it is true that this path may present challenges, each obstacle overcome will bring you closer to personal and professional fulfillment. Regardless of your profession, gender, age, origin, language or beliefs, opportunities in this field are available to everyone, there is always room to grow and learn in this exciting field. It's time to unlock your potential and write your own path to success in the world of data and technology!

If you are interested in training to take advantage of the opportunity to have a professional career in this sector, I will be happy to provide you with recommendations and additional resources. Do not hesitate to contact me through my website www.mujerseguridad.com or on the main social networks with the user @mujerseguridad! I'm here to help you develop your skills and advance your career in this exciting field.

EXTRA BONUS: 60 FACTS THEY WILL NEVER TELL YOU

Are you ready to unlock the unlimited potential of digital knowledge? As we conclude this exciting tour through the world of intelligence agencies, I want to thank you for your complicity in accompanying me. As a token of gratitude, I have a special gift for you: a bonus chapter full of practical and useful resources that are rarely shared.

In this chapter, you will discover how to make the most of the vast digital universe ethically and safely. From books and movies to applications and management tools, I will provide you with the keys to enrich your daily and professional experience.

Imagine having access to an infinite library of complete books at no cost. We'll explore platforms like Project Gutenberg and the Open Library, where you'll find literary treasures just a click away. Additionally, I'll introduce you to LibriVox, a global community of volunteers offering free audiobooks in multiple languages.

Are you a movie lover? You'll discover free streaming services like Tubi TV and Crackle, which will allow you to enjoy movies and series without spending a dime. We will also explore the most complete database of films in Spanish and the largest community of film buffs in Latin America.

And if you need technological tools, I will tell you about open-source software repositories like SourceForge and GitHub, where you will find educational and productivity applications at no cost. In addition, you will learn about social listening and consumer analytics platforms powered by artificial intelligence, ideal for managing and analyzing data safely.

If you are passionate about history and culture, I will guide you through platforms that offer access to cultural treasures and historical documents from around the world. From the " Wayback Machine", which archives websites, to virtual libraries that store digital books in various languages.

This chapter is more than just a list of resources; It is an invitation to explore and make the most of the knowledge available online. Feel the power to continue learning and growing, using tools that will help you achieve your goals efficiently and ethically.

Thank you for being part of this journey. Enjoy reading and keep learning!

How to watch complete movies and series for free

1. Tubi

Tubi is a completely free **streaming platform** that offers an alternative to services like Netflix and Amazon Prime Video. With an extensive catalog of more than 40 thousand titles and 64 million active users. Tubi offers a wide variety of movies and TV shows in genres ranging from horror and action to romance and family content. It is especially attractive to those interested in films, series and documentaries on intelligence, espionage, cybersecurity and related topics.

Tubi 's great advantage is its AVOD (Ad Supported Video-On-Demand) business model, which means that it offers content at no cost to the user, financed by advertising. This distinguishes it from platforms like Netflix and Amazon Prime, which require monthly payments. In addition, Tubi stands out for its curated library, that is, a carefully chosen selection of content, which includes a variety of films, series and documentaries in Spanish on intelligence, espionage, cybersecurity and related topics.

Although it may not have the same amount of content as some of its larger competitors, Tubi focuses on offering a high-quality viewing experience with titles relevant to its target audience.

2. Filmin

Filmin is an **online cinema platform** created in Spain that encourages interaction between users and offers personalized recommendations based on each user's viewing history and preferences. Its extensive catalog ranges from auteur and independent cinema to commercial productions. This allows those interested in the world of intelligence agencies to discover new films, series and documentaries on these topics effectively.

Although Filmin offers a selection of free content, it also has a paid subscription called Filmin Plus, which provides access to a larger catalog and additional features.

The free content on Filmin includes independent films and series, short films, documentaries and other types of content selected specifically for this modality. However, it is important to note that the availability of free movies may vary by region and content licensing agreements.

3. Amazon Prime Video

Amazon Prime Video is a **streaming platform** that presents a wide range of audiovisual content, including movies, television series, documentaries and original programs produced by Amazon Studios. Many of these titles address intriguing and complex aspects related to intelligence and espionage, offering a fresh and unique look at these topics.

It's available as part of an Amazon Prime subscription, which also includes additional benefits like fast and free shipping, access to music, e-books, and more. Amazon Prime Video is included as part of the Amazon Prime subscription, which costs annually or monthly. In addition, it has a 30-day free trial for new users, during which they can access Amazon Prime Video content and other Prime benefits at no cost.

Provides high-quality video streams, including content in 4K Ultra HD resolution and surround sound, for an immersive viewing experience. Although some titles may be available to rent or purchase separately, Amazon Prime still offers excellent value for money compared to other platforms.

4. AppleTV

Apple TV + is an Apple **streaming service that offers exclusive content produced by itself and other studios, with exceptional quality.** Its catalog includes series, movies, documentaries and children's programs. It stands out especially for those interested in intelligence, espionage and cybersecurity topics, as its original content deeply explores these areas in exciting ways. Additionally, Apple TV+ is ad-free and allows you to download content for offline viewing.

Although some options on Apple TV are free, most content requires a subscription to Apple TV+ and the individual purchase or rental of specific titles. However, the platform offers a free trial period for users to explore its catalog before committing to a subscription, making it an accessible option for those who want to immerse themselves in its content.

And don't forget that when you buy an Apple device, you get 3 free months of Apple TV+, an opportunity that shouldn't be missed. Make the most of this offer!

5. Rakuten TV

Rakuten TV is a **streaming platform** Japanese that offers a wide selection of movies, series and documentaries on demand. Although its focus is not exclusively on the world of intelligence agencies, its diverse catalog includes some of the best series and movies related to cybersecurity and technology, which may be relevant to this audience.

In addition to its paid content, Rakuten TV offers a catalog of free channels that broadcast 24 hours a day, although the option of premium content is available for those looking for a more complete experience. It stands out for its flexibility and convenience, as it allows you to rent or buy specific content individually, granting immediate access to a wide range of options, without having to commit to a monthly subscription and in some countries it offers a 1-month free trial.

Although users praise the ease of use and the availability of good movies, some point out aspects for improvement such as the duration of the rental and the lack of parental controls. If you are interested in exploring series and documentaries that address scientific or technological topics Rakuten TV could be an excellent option for you.

6. Google TV

Google TV is an **entertainment platform** that offers a unified viewing experience by integrating multiple streaming services and television channels, along with popular Google apps such as the Google Play Store, Alexa and YouTube.

With an extensive catalog that exceeds 400,000 movies, series and documentaries available to rent or buy on demand, Google TV also offers the FAST (Free Ad- Supported Streaming Television) modality, which provides access to more than 800 free channels without the need for a subscription. or paid, with more than 80,000 titles that include interspersed advertisements. Although its focus is not limited exclusively to content related to intelligence, espionage, and cybersecurity, its diverse catalog may contain titles relevant to this audience.

This platform is interesting due to the wide variety of content available, accessibility from any compatible device and the option to download purchased content to view offline. Google TV is available in several regions, although services may vary by location.

7. Tivify

Tivify is a Spanish **digital television** platform that brings together a wide selection of online television channels, both DTT (Digital Terrestrial Television) and other services, consolidating itself as a "platform of platforms". Although it does not generate its own content, it stands out for collecting the free broadcast of DTT channels and combining them with the flexibility of online transmission. It offers an experience adapted to the user's interests, with a variety of live television channel options, including thematic, children's, sports, regional and international, which could be attractive to an audience fond of espionage and intelligence topics.

Previously, Tivify was a premium service that required a monthly subscription, but now it also offers a free version that includes live content from these channels without ads or payments, maintaining the same resolution quality. In addition, it allows the recording of programs on mobile devices, computers and Smart TVs.

Tivify is presented as an interesting option for those looking for a wide variety of television channels, recording options and access to live content without additional costs. For an even more complete experience, Tivify Premium offers more recording options and access to premium channels. It is available in several countries and has a mobile application.

8. Pluto TV

Pluto TV is a completely free **streaming platform**, which operates under the format known as AVOD (Video on Demand with Ads), owned by Paramount Global and based in the United States. It offers a wide variety of online television channels where users can enjoy content continuously, similar to the traditional television experience, without the need to register. In addition, it has a mobile application available for iOS and Android devices.

With more than 80 million monthly active users worldwide, Pluto TV stands out by offering more than 100 specially selected thematic channels, available both live and on demand, with options for all tastes. The programming ranges from Cinema, Series and Novels to Realities, Children's Content and more.

Pluto TV also has exclusive documentary channels, such as crime and mystery channels, which could be attractive to audiences interested in intelligence, espionage and investigations. This diversity of content and the absence of costs for users make Pluto TV a very attractive option for those looking for free and varied entertainment online.

9. Hulu

Hulu is a **video-on-demand service** that offers a wide range of content, including streaming of recent television shows, movies, documentaries, and series from both the United States and Japan. It is compatible with various devices and has parental control options to ensure a safe environment.

Although its main audience is female, representing 52% of total subscriptions, Hulu stands out for its diversity of entertainment. It offers content in Spanish and Latin American productions, as well as movies, original series and popular television programs that can be enjoyed just 24 hours after their original broadcast.

Subscribers can access optional packages such as Disney+,

NFL RedZone and ESPN+, thus expanding the entertainment offering available. In addition, its content is geolocated and may vary depending on the region. According to statistics, about 34.7 million visitors use VPN services to bypass geo-blocking and access Hulu's international content. Depending on your location, you could qualify for a one-month free trial or, better yet, if you're a college student, get unlimited access to the entire library for a discounted rate.

10. Disney Plus

Disney+ is a **streaming service** owned by The Walt Disney Company that offers a wide range of multimedia content, including movies, series, documentaries and original programming from Disney, Pixar, Marvel, Star Wars and National Geographic. With more than 158 million subscribers globally.

For audiences interested in intelligence and related topics, Disney+ offers relevant content, especially through its franchise of spy films such as James Bond, as well as series and documentaries from National Geographic that explore topics of technology, intelligence and national security.

Disney+ allows some full access options to its catalog of movies, series and documentaries for free. You can take advantage of the 7-day free trial offered by Disney+. If you are located in Spain, Mexico and Latin America, you could opt for up to two months free on Disney Plus. In addition, some operators and cable companies may have other similar offers. Remember to check the availability of these options in your country and enjoy Disney+ content at no additional cost.

11. Star Plus

Star+ is a Disney **streaming service that stands out for its focus on a more adult and diverse audience, offering varied content on intelligence, espionage, cybersecurity and more.**

In addition to offering movies, series and documentaries, Star+ includes live sports broadcasts from ESPN, which differentiates it from other platforms.

With availability in Latin America, Star+ is presented as the equivalent of Hulu in the United States, offering a wide catalog that includes award-winning films and emblematic series from various entertainment brands. This allows it to offer a wider variety of genres and themes to satisfy the tastes of a more mature audience.

Currently, Star+ offers a temporary promotion called Star+ Free Pass, which allows users to access the platform's content free of charge for a limited period. During this time, subscribers can enjoy exclusive content, live ESPN sports matches, movies, series and original productions, providing a unique opportunity to explore the Star+ offering at no cost.

12. Vudu

Vudu is a Walmart-owned **video streaming service** that offers access to thousands of movie titles, series, TV shows, and original content for free, with no monthly subscription required.

This platform has one of the largest catalogs, with more than 20,000 movies and 8,000 TV shows. In addition to free content, it allows individual payment options for the specific movies or shows you want to watch, rather than a subscription.

You can watch Vudu on different devices, download the content and play it offline, with quality options including 1080p, 4K and Ultra HD. Although its main availability is focused on the United States and Canada, it is possible to access it in other territories by using a VPN due to geographic restrictions.

13. Netflix

Netflix is a leading global **streaming service platform**, known for its extensive catalog of content that includes series, movies and documentaries. It uses a monthly subscription video on demand (SVOD) model, offering users unlimited access to its content as long as their subscription is active.

It has a wide selection of titles in genres related to intelligence, espionage and technology, ranging from the intriguing series "House of Cards " to the disturbing "Black Mirror ". In addition, the platform has the ability to present personalized recommendations adjusted to the preferences of each user, making it easier to search and discover relevant and attractive content.

Although it doesn't offer an option to watch its content for free indefinitely, Netflix does provide a free trial subscription for new users for a limited period. And it provides the flexibility to change plans or cancel online at any time, without contracts, cancellation fees or commitments, with the peace of mind to try the platform and decide if they want to continue with the service.

Netflix has a significant global subscriber base of over 260 million users with 52% female and is available in most countries, except those where it is prohibited or restricted due to legal or regulatory issues.

14. HBO MAX

HBO Max is an American independent **streaming platform** that merges the best of HBO, Warner Bros., DC, Cartoon Network and more. Its catalog ranges from iconic films to award-winning series and Max Originals. For audiences interested in topics such as intelligence, espionage, cybersecurity and other related topics, HBO Max offers an extensive catalog, with more than 45,000 hours of entertainment and a wide selection of productions that explore these topics in a deep and captivating way.

Its competitive advantage lies in its partnership with HBO, which gives it access to exclusive, high-quality content, in addition to having a library of film and television classics. Its interface is easy to use and offers excellent image and sound quality.

In certain territories, some HBO Max providers may offer a free trial to new subscribers. During this free trial, users can stream all HBO Max content. If you enjoy the HBO Max experience, no action is required and your subscription will automatically renew each billing period until you decide to cancel.

15. SeriesLAN

SeriesLAN is an online platform that offers a wide catalog of cartoon series and nostalgic programs spanning various generations, from the late 70s to recent times. This platform can be accessed completely free through its Android application or directly from its website.

Access to the platform is free and the content is available to enjoy even without having a user account. Although SeriesLAN specializes in retro series and cartoons of European, Asian and North American origin, some of these may contain elements of espionage and adventure that offer a playful introduction to concepts related to espionage and intelligence.

It is one of the most complete platforms for collecting cartoons, series and programs dubbed into Spanish, which makes it likely that you will find your favorite childhood production there. In addition, it allows you to legally and free download the episodes of the series you want, which is very useful if you don't always have access to a stable Internet connection.

16. Plex

Plex is an **online entertainment platform** with global reach, notable for its free core functionality that includes streaming a wide variety of content, from movies and series to live TV shows. In addition, it offers more than 100 free channels with advertising content and an extensive library of 20,000 titles available on demand, offering a Netflix-like experience and combining personalization with cross-platform compatibility and download option for offline viewing.

For those interested in technological topics, state affairs, espionage and cybersecurity, Plex is an excellent option, allowing the organization and transmission of your own multimedia library, as well as integration with accounts from other platforms such as Hulu, Netflix, Max and Disney+. This provides a personalized and enriching viewing experience.

Although Plex offers a premium subscription called Plex Pass with additional features, much of its functionality is accessible for free, making it an attractive option for a wide range of users looking for a versatile and personalized entertainment experience.

17. Acontra

Acontra + is a **multi-platform streaming service** offering both subscription video on demand (SVOD) and transaction video on demand (TVOD), combining the excellence of cinema with the convenience of online content. This unique proposition not only promotes movie enjoyment at home, but also in movie theaters, and as an added benefit, gives away free movie tickets, for some countries.

Promoted by the independent Spanish distributor A Contracorriente Films, this initiative emerged as a virtual extension of movie theaters at a time of confinement, providing support to a highly affected sector. It is supported by the Recovery, Transformation and Resilience Plan of the European cultural industry.

Acontra + catalog ranges from classic film collections to family features, art documentaries, operas and ballets, as well as exciting titles that immerse viewers in intriguing plots and adventures. In addition, it offers the option to download the content to view it offline anywhere. In addition, they offer a 7-day free trial so you can discover their catalog without obligation.

18. JustWatch

JustWatch is a Germany-based **metasearch engine** that makes it easy to find movies and series to watch online. Indexes the catalogs of various legal streaming services, such as Netflix, HBO, Amazon Prime Video and Disney+. With more than 106,000 titles and based on the activity of more than 40 million users per month, JustWatch does not play content, but indicates where you can watch the titles on the appropriate platforms.

Its service is free and does not influence the prices of the platforms nor does it require registration. Offers trailers, synopsis, cast and ratings for each title. It is available in more than 120 countries and its catalog adapts to the user's geographic location. It is accessible from multiple devices and has a mobile application for greater convenience.

JustWatch 's personalization feature is an invaluable tool for those interested in exploring movies, series and documentaries on intelligence agencies, espionage, cybersecurity and related topics. It allows you to quickly find content related to these topics, create watchlists, receive personalized recommendations and be aware of new releases in this field, with detailed information about each title.

19. FilmAffinity

FilmAffinity is **the most important and complete database** of Spanish-language cinema on the Internet. Worldwide, it is recognized for being a reference in consulting user ratings and reviews for each film, series, documentary, short film and television program. In addition, FilmAffinity is an independent platform that allows you to vote and receive personalized movie recommendations based on each user's personal affinity.

This platform offers detailed information about the movies, as well as links to watch them on various streaming platforms, such as Netflix, HBO Max, Amazon Prime Video and others. Its active community, made up of more than 1 million registered users, shares opinions and reviews about each film production. This provides valuable insight into the quality and content of films related to topics such as intelligence, espionage, and cybersecurity.

FilmAffinity 's main focus is cinema, its extensive catalog also covers a wide range of series and documentaries related to these topics. If you are interested in exploring content related to intelligence and cybersecurity, FilmAffinity can be a useful tool for you.

20. Peliplat

Peliplat is a completely free Argentine online platform designed especially for movie lovers or those interested in a particular genre. It houses more than 3 million titles in Spanish, English and Portuguese, from classics to the latest releases. In addition, it has become **the largest community of film fans in Latin America,** with more than 1 million monthly visits and 900,000 user registrations. Its global reach allows you to connect with film lovers around the world.

But Peliplat is not limited to providing data on movies, documentaries, series, programs and more. It also offers a unique space for discussion and analysis on your topics of interest. Do you want to share your opinions about your favorite 007 agent? Or discuss female espionage filmography? Here you can do it!

This platform does not provide direct streaming services,

but you can get summaries, reviews, interesting facts, and recommendations. And if you prefer to write about cinema, Peliplat encourages you to publish articles related to your genres of interest. And best of all, you can earn up to $600 a month for your contributions!

21. BBC iPlayer

BBC iPlayer is an **online streaming service** developed by the BBC. It allows viewers to watch British television programs and listen to British radio programs over the Internet. The platform offers a wide variety of content, including series, movies, documentaries and entertainment programs. Unlike BBC America, which is a basic cable channel with programming for US audiences, BBC iPlayer is designed for UK audiences and offers free and convenient access to a selection of high-quality content, including intelligence-related topics., espionage and cybersecurity.

In addition, its competitive advantage is based on its extensive library of titles, the possibility of watching live programs and customization according to user preferences. Although its scope is limited to the United Kingdom, where the BBC is based, through the VPN network the platform allows access from abroad without major difficulties. With 4K quality programs, downloadable programs and a great interface compatible with multiple types of devices, iPlayer is a great option for those interested in exploring the world of British information and entertainment. You can watch it online and live from your computer or mobile device.

You can enjoy TV programs from the last seven days and listen to radio recordings up to 30 days old, in addition to accessing live broadcasts.

Applications and other resources to expand your Horizons

22. Hootsuite

Hootsuite, a **social media management platform,** supports a wide range of apps and services, including Facebook, Twitter, now X, Instagram, LinkedIn, YouTube, Pinterest, and more, as well as offering integrations with analytics tools. social networks, cloud storage, CRM and collaboration platforms. It allows users to schedule and publish content across multiple platforms, monitor mentions and conversations about their brand, analyze post performance, and collaborate with teams on social account management.

For intelligence analysts, Hootsuite represents a valuable tool by facilitating data collection, monitoring online trends and opinions, identifying potential threats or opportunities, as well as generating detailed reports, simplifying decision making. strategic.

As for its pricing model, Hootsuite offers a free version with limited basic functionality, as well as paid plans that provide access to more advanced features and specialized support.

23. Buffer

Buffer is another **online post management tool,** similar to Hootsuite, but much more convenient for small teams on a limited budget. For intelligence analysts, Buffer may be interesting for its ability to schedule and analyze social media posts efficiently, although Hootsuite may offer more advanced tools for real-time analysis and monitoring.

Buffer allows integrations with social media analysis tools such as Google Analytics or Bitly and is differentiated by its ease of use and focused approach to content programming. Its main advantage lies in its ability to simply and efficiently schedule posts on multiple platforms in advance. It offers a free version with limitations, but has subscription plans with more features and analytical data.

24. Brandwatch

Brandwatch is a **consumer analytics platform powered by artificial intelligence.** Unlike Hootsuite and Buffer, Brandwatch is not limited to just scheduling posts. Access 1.7 billion historical conversations since 2010, allowing you to understand trends and behaviors over time. Incorporates 501 million new conversations daily, keeping you updated. Access data from Twitter, now X, Tumblr, and Reddit to analyze organization brand perception.

It collects data from more than 100 million unique websites, enriching the analysis. It has Artificial Intelligence to offer instant perception diagnosis and image analysis.

Although its free version has limitations, its ease of use and compatibility with multiple social networks make it valuable for intelligence analysts. As for cons, Brandwatch can be complex for new users due to its wide range of features. Additionally, its cost can be high for small businesses or startups with limited budgets.

25. Sprout Social

Sprout Social stands out for its focus on comprehensive social media management, offering advanced analytics, **post scheduling,** and user engagement tools. Unlike Hootsuite and Buffer, Sprout Social places an emphasis on team collaboration and the ability to manage high volumes of social interactions.

Its advantages include an intuitive interface, detailed reports, and strong integration with social media analytics applications such as Google Analytics and Google Data Studio. Additionally, Sprout Social is compatible with a wide range of platforms and allows integration with analytics tools. This makes it an attractive option for intelligence analysts, as its customer-centric approach and ability to provide a complete view of social media performance allows them to make informed and strategic decisions.

26. Talkwalker

Talkwalker is a **social listening** and media analytics platform that allows brands to monitor, analyze and respond to online conversations about their brand, products or industry. It is extremely useful for intelligence analysts as it provides them with a deep understanding of audience perception, spotting trends, monitoring competitors, and evaluating the impact of marketing campaigns.

It is compatible with a variety of other apps and tools, including integrations with Google Analytics, Salesforce, Tableau, and more. It allows free trials and personalized plans according to the user's needs. Additionally, it allows integrations with social media analysis tools such as Brandwatch, Sysomos and Crimson. Hexagon, allowing users to get a complete view of the digital landscape.

27. Meltwater

Meltwater is a media monitoring and digital media analysis platform that allows you **to track online mentions,** analyze public perception and monitor people's opinion using artificial intelligence tools. With the ability to process up to ~1 billion pieces of content daily, Meltwater transforms this information into vital data.

For intelligence analysts, Meltwater is extremely useful. Provides valuable data for strategic decision making, identification of emerging trends and evaluation of brand performance. Additionally, its compatibility with tools such as Google Analytics, Slack, Microsoft Teams, Bit.ly, DingTalk, and generic Webhook allows for integrations with other social media analytics applications, such as Brandwatch, Sysomos, and Crimson. Hexagon. This expands its ability to provide a complete view of the digital landscape. Meltwater also offers free demos and customized plans based on each client's needs.

28. Crimson hexagon

Crimson Hexagon is a social media analytics platform that uses natural language processing (NLP), machine learning and neural networks to **understand public perception,** identify trends, perceive sentiments and measure the impact of public opinion on social media, in real time.

For the intelligence sector, Crimson Hexagon is valuable due to its ability to track and analyze data in real time, as well as its integration with social media analysis tools. Its focus on social intelligence and deep understanding of data make it an attractive option for making informed and strategic decisions about target audiences.

29. Palantir

Palantir has a comprehensive approach to intelligence and is used to manage and **analyze data securely and responsibly.** This platform allows you to integrate, visualize and analyze large amounts of data from various sources to obtain meaningful information and make informed decisions.

For intelligence services, Palantir is valuable because of its ability to track and analyze complex and heterogeneous data, identify patterns and relationships, and provide intuitive visualizations in real time. In addition, its integration with social media analysis tools, such as Google Analytics, Slack, Microsoft Teams, Bit.ly, DingTalk and generic Webhook, among others, makes it an attractive option widely used in the government sphere.

30. Dataminr

Dataminr is a **social media intelligence tool** used to track, detect, analyze and **alert in real time** about important events such as natural disasters, crises, protests, financial news and others. It uses artificial intelligence and data analysis to identify relevant and emerging information from public sources on social networks, news and other online media.

Provides early warnings about situations that could affect emerging trends and that may have national security implications. This allows analysts to make quick, data-driven decisions to mitigate risks or capitalize on opportunities. Although it does not offer a full free version, you can request a demo to explore its capabilities.

31. NC4

NC4 is an **intelligence and risk management platform** used to collect, analyze and share security information in real time. It allows institutions to prevent and respond to threats and crises. It is very useful because it provides security intelligence solutions for governments and organizations, offering them critical data on events and situations that may affect national security or the continuity of operations. This includes social media analytics for threat detection and real-time event monitoring.

Additionally, it is valuable to intelligence agencies due to its focus on security and data protection. NC4 is also compatible with a variety of other incident management applications, tools and systems, as well as risk analysis tools.

32. Geofeedia

Geofeedia is a **location intelligence platform** that allows you to collect, visualize and analyze geospatial information and social media content in real time. This tool, unlike Dataminr, focuses on monitoring events, activities, and trends in specific geographic locations, which is useful for various sectors such as security, marketing, and emergency management.

For intelligence services, Geofeedia is valuable, due to its ability to track and analyze in real time, events and activities that are occurring in specific locations, identify emerging trends, detect potential threats and perform situation analysis, to take timely actions.

33. Media Sonar

Media Sonar is an internet and **social media intelligence platform** used to monitor, filter, aggregate, collect and analyze information from millions of online contents efficiently. It helps organizations identify potential threats, assess security risk, manage online reputation, and detect suspicious activity on the web and on location-based, non-geolocated social networks that are published daily.

For intelligence analysts, Media Sonar can be an extremely useful tool, providing them with access to real-time data on online events and trends that may have implications for the organization's security and reputation. It allows analysts to drill down into information and uncover hidden connections between different events and entities.
Provides free demos and trials for potential customers.

34. Sysomos

Sysomos is used by some government agencies to monitor and review conversations on multiple social media platforms about topics of public interest. This **social listening and analytics platform** is used to understand public perception, interpret sentiment in real time, identify emerging trends, and measure the impact of public relations strategies.

Sysomos provides data and metrics that can be useful to intelligence analysts, offering a detailed, real-time view of how the public is responding to certain events, topics or campaigns on social media. This allows you to identify opportunities, threats and potential challenges. Although it does not offer a full free version, demos can be requested to explore its capabilities.

35. Tableau

Tableau is a **data analysis and visualization platform** which allows users to create interactive visualizations and dashboards from data stored in different sources, such as databases, spreadsheets, and cloud services. It serves to explore and analyze data intuitively, identify patterns, trends and relationships, and communicate findings effectively.

It is ideal for monitoring emerging trends and patterns, as it offers connectors and extensions that allow integration with social media platforms such as Facebook, Twitter, now X, and LinkedIn, among others. Its visualization capabilities, advanced analytics, and flexibility in integration with other tools make Tableau an attractive option. Its focus on social intelligence and deep understanding of data make it an attractive option for intelligence analysts.

36. Dome

Domo is a **data analysis and visualization platform** that has an intuitive interface, designed to collect, prepare, present and share relevant data in real time. This tool optimizes information management, facilitating strategic decision making.

In the field of intelligence, it is revealed as an invaluable resource due to its effectiveness in the analysis of large volumes of data and its ability to communicate it in a visually attractive way. This is essential for identifying trends, patterns and relationships in the data, which can lead to meaningful discoveries and the implementation of strategic actions. Although it does not have a permanently free version, it offers free demos and trials for interested users.

37. QlikView

QlikView is an **advanced business intelligence solution** designed for interactive data analysis and visualization. It makes it easy for users to upload information from multiple sources and allows them to explore relationships between different data sets, resulting in deeper insights and making informed decisions in a timely manner.

Although it does not support direct integrations with social media platforms for real-time analysis of social data, QlikView provides government institutions with a powerful tool for data analysis, contributing to the improvement of transparency and efficiency, supporting effective management of public resources.

How to read and download books legally

38. 5books

5libros is a platform that offers free access to **lists of recommended books** in different literary genres and themes, including crime novels, political thrillers, and spy novels. Additionally, it has a significant selection of content in Spanish, making it accessible to Spanish-speaking readers.

The content of 5libros may be interesting to you if you are interested in learning about espionage and intelligence, as it offers lists of books dedicated to espionage fiction, with titles that explore the "world of secrecy", from the time before the First World War to the present. These books can provide a fascinating and entertaining insight into modern intelligence agencies and services and covert operations.

39. InfoLibros.org

InfoLibros.org is an online library that offers free access to an extensive and updated **catalog of books in PDF format.** Designed to satisfy the passion for reading and knowledge at no cost. At InfoLibros.org, you can find books on a variety of topics, including classic literature, science, philosophy, art, languages, and more. that could contain books related to espionage and intelligence. In addition, the page provides lists of the most downloaded books and allows fast downloading without registration.

If you are interested in exploring their collection or want more information on how to access the books, you can visit their official website. It is a valuable resource for readers of all ages and diverse interests, especially for those seeking to expand their knowledge or enjoy literature without incurring expenses.

40. PlanetaLibros.net

PlanetaLibro.net is a **virtual library** that allows you **to read free books online and also download them.** Its catalog has more than 70,000 titles, including 15,000 public domain books. They have a wide variety of genres, from novels to science fiction, fantasy, literature for children and adolescents, history, classics and romance.

The content of PlanetaLibros.net could be interesting to learn about espionage, intelligence and related topics. Many works on the site explore espionage plots, offering an entertaining and engaging view of this world. Due to its wide variety of genres and authors, you are likely to find different perspectives on the topic of espionage and intelligence.

41. European Digital Library

The Europeana Digital Library is an online platform that provides free access to a large number of European **cultural and heritage resources.** Offers a wide variety of digitized content, including books, photographs, manuscripts, art, music, audio and video files, and much more.

Its content is relevant to learning about espionage, intelligence and related topics due to its wide range of cultural and heritage resources related to historical events, conflicts and European geopolitics. From historical documents to photographs, art and literature, they can provide unique perspectives on intelligence and espionage strategies over time, allowing for rich analysis from diverse historical and cultural perspectives.

42. World Digital Library

The World Digital Library is a collaborative project that brings together **cultural treasures and historical documents from around the world.** In it, you will find a vast collection of books, photographs, maps, recordings and historical documents. It is an initiative of UNESCO and the United States Library of Congress that offers free access, including to ancient manuscripts, rare books, historical maps, photographs, audio and video recordings, and newspapers.

This free access facilitates the exploration and study of topics such as espionage and intelligence by providing a wide range of historical documents that can offer global perspectives on such matters, allowing researchers to examine events and activities related to espionage in different periods of more of 10,000 years of history and in diverse cultures and languages.

43. Miguel de Cervantes Virtual Library

The Miguel de Cervantes Virtual Library is a pioneering project in the Spanish language that houses a vast bibliographic collection. Here you will find works of Literature, History, Science, and more. Access is completely free and
You can **legally download thousands of digital books** on linguistics, classic and contemporary literature, history, art, science and more. In addition, access the digital lending platform to discover titles from publishers around the world and participate in virtual reading and film clubs.

The library offers professionally narrated Spanish audiobooks, databases, dictionaries, encyclopedias and other electronic materials. In addition, its diverse content can provide historical and cultural context on topics such as espionage and intelligence, allowing the analysis of literary works and historical documents related to these topics.

44. Project Gutenberg

Project Gutenberg is an initiative that collects and distributes copyright-free books in several languages, including Spanish. This digital library **offers free and legal access to more than 70,000 books in various languages.** In the Spanish section, you can find literary classics, works by renowned authors, audiobooks, images and music. In addition, it gives you the opportunity to collaborate with the project. Its objective is to provide free access to literary and educational works through the Internet from anywhere in the world.

Although it does not focus specifically on espionage and intelligence topics, its extensive collection includes fundamental works in these fields, such as historical treatises on espionage tactics, intelligence analysis, and biographies of relevant figures in the field of national security.

45. Internet Archive

Internet Archive is a **virtual library that stores websites** and other cultural artifacts in digital format. Its main objective is to preserve digital files of global interest. Founded as a non-profit organization in 1996, this platform stores millions of books, audios, videos, movies, audiobooks, software, newspapers, declassified documents, government reports and much more, in various languages. All content is free and legal, making it an excellent source for researching and learning about various topics, including espionage, intelligence, and other related fields.

With collaborative projects such as OpenLibrary, this portal has become one of the most important digital repositories on the planet. Because it allows you to enjoy online or download all its content from any country. Additionally, anyone with a free account can collaborate by uploading multimedia material to the platform. But its best tool is the iconic **"Wayback Machine"**, where you can get data from the past, exploring more than 866 billion web pages saved over time and going back to what they published, even if the page no longer exists. currently.

46. Wikisource

Wikisource is a collaborative project of the Wikimedia Foundation that hosts a large **collection of original and translated texts in any language.** All content is free and legal to access and use, as it is published under licenses such as GFDL (GNU Free Documentation License), free software licenses, Creative Commons or are public domain works. In Spanish, you can find a variety of content, including classic literature, historical documents, essays, laws, and more.

In relation to espionage, intelligence, and related topics, Wikisource can be a valuable source of declassified documents, international treaties, government reports, and other primary sources that offer detailed insight into the history and practice of intelligence and national security. You can also explore how espionage worked during the Cold War, the intelligence fight between the United States and the Soviet Union, and the technological advances used in surveillance and acquiring secrets.

47. Amazon Kindle

Amazon Kindle is a **digital reading platform** that offers a wide selection of e-books in multiple languages, including Spanish. In it, you can find a variety of content, from classic literary works to contemporary books and specialized texts. Although some books have a cost, the platform has a huge catalog of free books available for download legally, which often go unnoticed by users.

Public domain books are works that are no longer protected by copyright and therefore you can legally access them for free on various platforms, including Amazon's Kindle. This collection includes a wide range of classic literature, from works by Shakespeare to novels by Dickens and Austen, as well as historical and scientific texts. These books are a great way to access a wealth of knowledge and culture without breaking your budget. Additionally, on topics such as espionage, intelligence, technology, and cybersecurity, they can provide valuable historical insight through military treaties, spy stories, and other relevant texts.

48. AppleBooks

Apple Books is a **digital reading platform** developed by Apple with a wide selection of e-books and audiobooks in multiple languages, including Spanish. In it, you can find everything from contemporary bestsellers to literary classics, as well as non-fiction, academic and specialized or research books, biographies of agents and leaders, analysis of historical cases and intelligence techniques, providing a broad and enriching vision on various topics of interest to its millions of readers.

Although it is a paid subscription, for every new device you set up, they offer you a free trial of Apple Books for a specific period, which you may not have taken advantage of. Additionally, the platform has a store tab called "Our selection of free books ". It is a huge catalog that they constantly update, to enjoy online or download legally at no cost.

49. LibriVox

LibriVox is an **online library of free audiobooks in 47 different languages,** created by volunteers around the world who record readings of books that are out of copyright or already in the public domain. It is considered an "acoustic liberation" project, with the mission of making books also accessible through listening.

As of February 2023, there were 42,919 audiobooks available to listen to and download in MP3 formats. Although a high percentage of the collection is in English, Spanish is the fourth language with the greatest presence on the platform, with more than 900 titles of all literary genres, allowing users to enjoy their favorite works. Additionally, LibriVox accepts volunteers to read free audiobooks in the public domain, which can be a fascinating experience if you have the time and talent and interest to contribute to this worthy cause.

50. EBiblio

EBiblio is a **Spanish digital platform** that opens the doors to a world of knowledge, offering free and legal access to a wide variety of content. From e-books and audiobooks to magazines and newspapers, everything is available to card-carrying public library users. You can enjoy these resources on any device, thanks to a service promoted by the Ministry of Education, Culture and Sports, in collaboration with the autonomous communities.

In eBiblio you will find materials in Spanish on a multitude of topics, from literature and science to history and specialties such as espionage and intelligence. This last category is especially fascinating, with works that immerse you in the history, techniques, and cases of espionage, giving you a solid foundation for learning about these intriguing topics. With the support of the public library system, eBiblio ensures you quality and completely legal content.

51. Domínio Público BR

This portal is a **virtual library** managed by the Brazilian Ministry of Education. It offers free access to an incredible collection of more than 123 thousand works, including texts, sounds, images and videos that are in the public domain or whose disclosure has been authorized. Since its launch in 2004, it has become the largest virtual library in Brazil.

Domínio Público BR, puts at your disposal literary, artistic and scientific productions, such as the complete works of Machado de Assis, the rich Brazilian scholarly music, the moving poetry of

Fernando Pessoa, and children's literature in Portuguese, among many other gems. It is an invaluable resource for students, researchers and anyone eager to explore a wide range of cultural and educational content. If you want to explore their collection, you can visit their website and search for works by category, author, title, or language.

52. Z-Library

Z-Library is a **file sharing platform** which offers access to articles from academic journals, educational texts and books of general interest. It originated as a mirror of Library Genesis, but most of its books come from individual user contributions, with the mission of making literature accessible to as many people as possible. This has led to some copyright lawsuits and, on more than one occasion, they have faced domain restrictions or had to remove protected material.

This portal allows free access to an immense variety of content in almost all languages, available in PDF, ePub or audio format. You'll find literary genres ranging from fiction to nonfiction, including classics, poetry, essays, and more. In addition, there is a special section for children and young people, as well as magazines, newspapers and documents in Spanish. If you are interested in learning about espionage and intelligence, you can explore related works within its extensive catalog.

53. Elejandria

Elejandria is a web portal that allows you **to download free books by great authors** in PDF, EPUB and MOBI formats legally. All books available in Alexandria are in the public domain or have open licenses. Most titles are in Spanish, but it also offers a good selection of works in English, French, German and Italian, ranging from classic to contemporary literature, including authors such as Cervantes, Calderón de la Barca, Shakespeare and Jane Austen.

In addition, you will find carefully selected collections, such as writers who marked history or books that have been adapted to film. Although it does not specialize in topics of espionage and intelligence, Elejandria provides a valuable opportunity to explore these fields of study, as it includes historical texts and novels that address these topics from various perspectives.

54. Google Books

Google Books or "Google Books" is a service that allows you **to search, read and buy books online** from anywhere in the world, in multiple languages and devices. Google has 25 million books in its database, among which there are thousands that have become public domain or were freely accessible from the beginning, and which can be read online or downloaded at no cost.

Additionally, Google Books provides excerpts and previews of even copyrighted books, allowing you to explore the content before deciding to purchase or access full versions that may be available on other portals mentioned in this book. This combination of free and legal access makes Google Books a valuable tool for obtaining publications in any area of interest.

55. Texts.info

Textos.info is an open digital library that functions as **a free publishing platform for authors and publishers.** It allows full access from any device with an Internet connection to its interesting catalog, which has more than 4,000 titles by more than 500 authors. Users can search, read, share, rate, comment and download books legally and at no cost.

Textos.info allows authors to publish and share their works to make themselves known freely and maintain direct and continuous contact with their readers, generating an easy, accessible and free meeting point. Its catalog includes classic literature, as well as works by contemporary authors such as

Gabriel García Márquez and Julio Cortázar, as well as non-fiction works, plays, essays, academic texts and more. In short, any text, whatever its nature, orientation or ideology, has a place in Textos.info to be communicated and shared freely.

56. Dominican Digital Library

The Dominican Digital Library is the **digital portal of Dominican heritage**, created in 2018 by the Pedro Henríquez Ureña National Library, with the purpose of storing, preserving and facilitating the dissemination and access to the national bibliographical and intellectual wealth, originating both inside and outside the country. It offers free, legal access to more than 12,300 books, available for online reading or download.

Its collection covers various topics, with special attention to social sciences and history. If you are curious about espionage or intelligence in times of dictators or military invasions, intelligence and related topics, you could explore the books available in this library to find relevant material in Spanish. However, please note that the specific selection of titles related to those topics will depend on availability in the digital collection.

57. Dominican Books in PDF

Dominican Books in PDF is an initiative dedicated to the **dissemination of books** that promote Dominican themes and characters, regardless of the language of the text or the nationality of its author. This digital library works on a blog-type platform and its access is completely free for both authors and users. It has an extensive catalog of **out-of-print Dominican books**, which are difficult to find.

Among its most interesting works are "Dominican History from the Aborigines to the April War", "Military History of Santo Domingo", and an almost complete collection of everything that has been written about Juan Pablo Duarte, among many others. The main objective of the platform is to disseminate knowledge and information, considering them common, collective and universal goods, while promoting the protection of copyright. This initiative seeks to preserve the national historical memory and allow access to the Dominican cultural heritage from anywhere in the world.

58. Dialnet

Dialnet is an **open information system** which offers free and legal access to more than 9 million indexed academic resources from various areas of knowledge, with special emphasis on social sciences and history. This includes journals, theses and other materials, of which more than 570,000 are books

Dialnet's content is useful for students and researchers interested in topics such as espionage, intelligence, cybersecurity and related topics. This is because the platform hosts academic works and specialized analyzes that provide detailed and well-researched perspectives on these fields. Additionally, a high percentage of the multidisciplinary content in this database is available in full text and in Spanish.

59. DOAB

The DOAB, or Directory of Open Access **Academic Content Electronic Books,** is a peer-reviewed book location service that offers free, legal access for non-commercial use to the metadata of more than 26,000 open access books, from 370 editors and distributed in 17 multidisciplinary subject areas in any language.

On this portal, you can find content in Spanish related to various branches of knowledge, including social sciences, history, politics and more. Regarding intelligence and related areas, the DOAB offers a selection of books that address these topics from a rigorous academic perspective, providing detailed analysis, informed research and different theoretical approaches.

60. LISANews

LISANews is a **portal specialized in news and analysis** on geopolitics, intelligence, cybersecurity, criminology and human rights, promoted by the LISA Institute. Publish content in multiple languages, allowing a global audience to access critical and relevant information.

The site offers free, legal access to a variety of content, including in-depth analyses, how-to guides and reports from industry experts. In addition, it has a weekly newsletter that highlights the most important news in the fields of security, intelligence, cybersecurity, geopolitics and emergencies. They also have a podcast called "LISA Code", where the most important aspects of the geopolitics and intelligence panorama are explained in a simple and accessible way.

CONCLUSION

As we close the pages of "What an Intelligence Agency Will Never Tell You: 60 Key Facts", we gain a deeper, more nuanced understanding of the covert world of intelligence. From its history and purpose to contemporary challenges and future opportunities, this book has been an eye-opening journey through the entanglements of intelligence agencies.

We learned that intelligence agencies are much more than shadowy entities; they are vital organisms that protect and serve society, operating under principles of necessity and proportionality. Espionage, far from being a relic of the past, remains essential in a world where data is as valuable as oil.

The pillars of intelligence - data collection, analysis and generation - have been revealed as the foundation on which global security is built. Counterespionage, counterterrorism, and cyber intelligence operations are essential to protecting nations from threats both old and new.

However, with power comes responsibility and the need for transparency. Ethical and legal challenges, along with big data management, require a delicate balance between security and privacy. Accountability is not just an ideal; It is a practice that ensures that power is not exercised without limits.

As we look to the future, intelligence is not only trendy, but a promising career path for those talented in data analysis. With online training resources and scholarships available, there has never been a better time to enter this dynamic and essential field.

This book has been more than a collection of facts; has been a guide to understanding the critical importance of intelligence agencies in our daily lives and how each of us can contribute to this field. With the additional resources and key data that I have provided, I hope that readers can equip themselves to continue their exploration and perhaps even join the next generation of spies or intelligence analysts, as they prefer.

If you feel like sharing your thoughts or discussing this topic further, I would be happy to hear from you. You can do so in the review of this book on Amazon, on my website www.mujerseguridad.com or by sending me a message on the main social networks with the user @mujerseguridad. Together we can explore the complexities of electronic monitoring and contribute to a safer and more ethical digital future for all.

ADDITIONAL RESOURCES

Recommended books:

1. *"The Secret World: A History of Intelligence"* - Christopher Andrew, 2019 https://amzn.to/4afRFjx
2. *"Intelligence: From Secrets to Policy"* - Mark M. Lowenthal, 2019 https://books.google.com.do/books?id=Fk6YDwAAQBAJ
3. *"The Orange Seller"* - Blanca Miosi, 2021 https://amzn.to/43WFs1a
4. *"The Spy"* - A Espiã | Paulo Coelho, 2017 https://amzn.to/3PFEiko
5. *"Spy School"* - Stuart Gibbs, 2020 https://amzn.to/3PLHWcO and the complete series https://amzn.to/3IZTAgo
6. *"Tinker Tailor Soldier Spy"* - El Topo | John le Carré, 2014 https://amzn.to/3IYWLoo
7. *"The Craft of Intelligence"* - Allen W. Dulles, 1963 https://amzn.to/3J2st4h
8. *"Secrets of Navajo Code Talkers"* - Rachael L. Thomas, 2023 https://amzn.to/4cC8Ayw
9. *"Spy Women: Intrigues and Sabotage Behind Enemy Lines"* - Laura Manzanera, 2008 https://amzn.to/3TXSEPG
10. *"InvestiGators: Agents of S.U.I.T."* - John Patrick Green, 2020. English version https://amzn.to/3xpl8Ji

Spanish version https://amzn.to/3TVujtQ
11. *"Legacy of Ashes: The Story of the CIA"* - Tim Weiner, 2007 https://amzn.to/3VKSm09
12. *"Los Hombres de la Niebla"* - Pablo Zarrabeitia, 2022 https://amzn.to/3J1Danw
13. *"El Agente Oscuro: Memorias de un espía infiltrado por el CNI"* - Anonymous Anonymous et al., 2019 https://amzn.to/3PL7Zkl
14. *"Inés y la Alegría"* - Almudena Grandes, 2010 https://amzn.to/43WiA1P
15. *"How to Be a Spy"* - Daniel Nesquens, 2022 https://amzn.to/3xvaf97
16. *"The Looming Tower: Al-Qaeda and the Roads to 9/11"* - Lawrence Wright, 2006 https://amzn.to/3TYFsZZ
17. *"Data and Goliath: The Hidden Battles to Collect Your Data and Control Your World"* - Bruce Schneier, 2016 https://amzn.to/49i9SvL
18. *"A Heart So White"* - Javier Marías, 1999 https://amzn.to/3VYjn0f
19. *"Espías al Galope"* - Berry Bees Book | Cat Le Blanc, 2020 https://amzn.to/4cIDLZ7
20. *"Marita: The Spy Who Loved Castro"* - Marita Lorenz, 2015 https://amzn.to/49wIzxP
21. *"Failure of Intelligence: The Decline and Fall of the CIA"* – Melvin A. Goodman, 2008 https://amzn.to/3PYbNig
22. *"Accountability and the Law"* - Transparency and Accountability versus Secrecy in Intelligence Operations | Arianna Vedaschi, 2021 https://doi.org/10.4324/9781003168331
23. *"Intelligence and Surprise Attack: Failure and Success from Pearl Harbor to 9/11 and Beyond"* - Erik J. Dahl, 2013 https://amzn.to/3THSxGP
24. *"The Code Book: The Secret History of Codes and Code-Breaking"* -Simon Singh, 1999 in English https://amzn.to/3VCOsWP free in Spanish: The secret codes - Simon Singh (librosmaravillosos.com)

25. **"God's Spy"** - Juan Gómez-Jurado, 2022 https://amzn.to/3Ua0NRg
26. **"8 Suspects, One Culprit"** - Actus Deouf, 2023 https://amzn.to/3J9TDGj

Suggested movies

1. **"The Good Shepherd"** | USA, 2006
2. **"The Catcher Was a Spy"** | USA, 2018
3. **"Munich"** | USA, 2005
4. **"Spy Game"** | USA, 2001
5. **"The spy next door"** | USA, 2010
6. *"Tinker Tailor Soldier Spy"* - El Topo | United Kingdom, 2012
7. **"SEAL Team Six"** - Code Gerónimo: The Hunt for Bin Laden | USA, 2012
8. **"True Lies"** | USA, 1994
9. **"Ghosted"** | USA, 2023
10. **"My Spy"** | USA, 2020
11. **"Agents 355"** | USA, 2022
12. **"Topaz"** | USA, 1969
13. **"Zero Dark Thirty"** - Darkest Night: Hunt for Osama Bin Laden | USA, 2012
14. **"Black Book"** | HOL, 2006
15. **"Notorious"** | USA, 1946
16. **"The Imitation Game"** | USA, 2014
17. **"The Family"** - A Dangerous Family | USA, 2013
18. **"Spies in Disguise"** | USA, 2019
19. **"Salt"** | USA, 2010
20. **"Get Smart"** - Get Smart | USA, 2008
21. **"Erin Brockovich"** | USA, 2000
22. **"The Lives of Others"** | Germany, 2006
23. **"A Call to Spy"** | USA, 2019
24. **"The Operative"** | FRA, 2019
25. **"Spy"** | USA, 2015

Unmissable series

1. **"The Looming Tower"** (USA, 2018)
2. **"The Bureau"** - Le Bureau des Légendes | Insider Office (FRA, 2015)
3. **"Spooks"** - Military Intelligence 5 "MI-5"| Double identity: Check on MI5 (UK, 2015)
4. **"Alias"** (USA, 2001)
5. **"The Americans"** | The infiltrators (USA, 2013)
6. **"Patriot"** (USA, 2017)
7. **"Burn Notice"** - Latest Notice | Stuck in Miami | Operation Miami (USA, 2007)
8. **"Homeland"** | Prisoner of War (USA, 2011)
9. **"Hatufim"** - Prisoners of War | Prisoner of War (ISR, 2011)
10. **"Danger Mouse"** The Justice Mouse (UK, 1981)
11. **"The Missiles of October"** - (USA, 1974)
12. **"War Spies"** (UK, 2019)
13. **"The Night Manager"** - The Infiltrator | (UK/USA, 2016)
14. **"Mrs. Wilson"** (UK, 2018)
15. **"Carmen Sandiego"** (USA, 2016)
16. **"Counterpart"** - Parallel Lives (USA, 2016)
17. **"Berlin Station"** (USA, 2016)
18. **"Covert Affairs"** (USA, 2010)
19. **"Killing Eve"** (USA, 2018)
20. **"KC Undercover"** (USA, 2015)
21. **"Eye in the Sky"** (HKG, 2015)
22. **"Rubicon"** (USA, 2010)
23. **"Condor"** (USA, 2018)
24. **"Alex Rider"** (UK, 2020)
25. **"Totally Spies!"** - KC Special Agent (FRA-CAN, 2001)

Online training portals

1. **Coursera** Coursera | Degrees, Certificates, & Free Online Courses https://www.coursera.org/
2. **Udemy** Online courses: learn everything at your own

pace | Udemy https://www.udemy.com/es/
3. **LinkedIn Learning** Train your employees and keep their skills up to date | LinkedIn Learning Solutions https://learning.linkedin.com/es-es
4. **edX** Free online courses from Harvard, MIT and more | edX https://www.edx.org/es
5. **Women4Cyber Academy** W4C Academy – Women4Cyber Academy https://women4cyberacademy.eu/

Scholarship platforms

1. **Scholarship Portal** Find Scholarships to Finance Your Study - ScholarshipPortal https://www.scholarshipportal.com/
2. **Scholarships.com** Find Scholarships for College https://www.scholarships.com/
3. **Becasyconvocatorias.org** Scholarships and calls for Latin Americans - ByC
4. **Sin Fronteras Scholarships** University of Toronto Lester B. Pearson International Scholarship Program, 2024 (becas-sin-fronteras.com) https://becas-sin-fronteras.com/
5. **Australia:** Australia Awards Scholarship Program Australia Awards Scholarships | Australian Government Department of Foreign Affairs and Trade (dfat.gov.au) https://www.dfat.gov.au/
6. **Brazil:** Ciência sem Fronteiras Program Ciência Sem Fronteiras — National Council for Scientific and Technological Development (www.gov.br) https://www.gov.br/
7. **Canada :** Emerging Leaders in the Americas Program (ELAP) Emerging Leaders in the Americas Program (ELAP) (educanada.ca) https://www.educanada.ca/
8. **China:** Chinese Government Scholarship (CSC) and Ministry of Education (MOE) International

Student Scholarship Program CSC Scholarships | China Scholarship Council | Chinese Government Scholarships (chinesescholarshipcouncil.com) https://www.chinesescholarshipcouncil.com/es/

9. **Spain:** Fundación Carolina and MAEC-AECID Scholarship Program Fundación Carolina - Home page - Fundación Carolina (fundacioncarolina.es) https://www.fundacioncarolina.es/

10. **United States:** Fulbright Program and International Student Scholarship Program (ISB) US Fulbright Program - Home Page (fulbrightonline.org) https://us.fulbrightonline.org/

11. **India:** University Grants Council of India (UGC). Welcome to UGC, New Delhi, India https://www.ugc.gov.in/

12. **Israel:** Israel Government Scholarship and MASHAV Scholarship MFA Scholarships for international students (academic year 2023-2024) | Ministry of Foreign Affairs (www.gov.il) https://www.gov.il/en/

13. **Japan:** Government of Japan Scholarship Program (Monbukagakusho). MEXT Scholarship for 2025 Embassy Recommendation | Study in Japan Official Website https://www.studyinjapan.go.jp/en/

14. **Ministry of Higher Education, Science and Technology (MESCYT)** Scholarship for your future | Your talent grows, the country grows (becas.gob.do) https://becas.gob.do/

15. **Organization of the American States (OAS)** "OAS Intelligence Studies Scholarship Program", "OAS Telecommunications Scholarships", the "OAS Cyberwomen Scholarship Program" and the "OAS Cybersecurity Professional Development Scholarships" OAS :: Scholarships (oas.org) https://www.oas.org/es/scholarships/

16. **Organization of Nations United Nations (UN):** "United *Nations Fellowships Programme* ", " ITU

Scholarship Programme ", the *" UN Cybersecurity Training Programme ", the "UN Cyberwoman "* and the *" UN Intelligence and Security Training Programme "*. training.dss.un.org - Online courses by the United Nations Department of Safety & Security https://training.dss.un.org/

17. **European Union:** Programs such as *"Erasmus Mundus"* Erasmus Mundus joint masters (students) - Erasmus+ (europa.eu) https://erasmus-plus.ec.europa.eu/es/
"Marie Skłodowska -Curie Actions (MSCA)" Home - Marie Skłodowska-Curie Actions (europa.eu) https://marie-sklodowska-curie-actions.ec.europa.eu/?etrans=en
"EU Cybersecurity Programme" European Cybersecurity Competence Center and Network (europa.eu) https://cybersecurity-centre.europa.eu/index_en

18. **Carlos Slim Foundation** scholarships - Carlos Slim Foundation | Carlos Slim Foundation (fundacioncarlosslim.org) https://fundacioncarlosslim.org/
19. **Fulbright Foundation** Experience of Studying in the USA (state.gov) https://educationusa.state.gov/
20. **Rockefeller Foundation** RF | Home (rockefellerfoundation.org) https://www.rockefellerfoundation.org/
21. **Open Society Foundation** Grants and Fellowships from the Open Society Foundations - Open Society Foundations
22. **Google** Build your future with Google https://buildyourfuture.withgoogle.com/scholarships
23. **Microsoft** Microsoft Learn: Develop skills that open doors in your career https://learn.microsoft.com/es-mx/

Platforms to watch complete movies and series for free

1. **Tubi** https://gdpr.tubi.tv/

2. Filmin https://www.filmin.es/
3. Amazon Prime Video https://www.primevideo.com/
4. Apple TV https://www.apple.com/la/apple-tv-plus/
5. Rakuten TV https://www.rakuten.tv/es
6. Google TV https://tv.google/intl/es_es/
7. Tivify www.tivify.es
8. Pluto TV https://pluto.tv/
9. Hulu www.hulu.com
10. Disney Plus https://www.disneyplus.com/
11. Star Plus https://www.starplus.com/
12. Vudu https://www.vudu.com/
13. Netflix https://www.netflix.com/
14. HBO MAX https://www.max.com/
15. SeriesLAN https://serieslan.com/
16. Plex https://www.plex.tv/es/
17. Acontra https://acontraplus.com/
18. JustWatch https://www.justwatch.com/es
19. Filmaffinity https://www.filmaffinity.com/es
20. Peliplat https://www.peliplat.com/es
21. BBC iPlayer https://www.bbc.co.uk/iplayer
22. VIX https://vix.com/

Portals to read and download books legally

23. 5libros https://5libros.net/

24. InfoLibros.org https://infolibros.org/

25. PlanetaLibros.net https://planetalibro.net/

26. Europeana Digital Library https://www.europeana.eu/es

27. World Digital Library https://www.loc.gov/

28. Miguel de Cervantes Virtual Library https://www.cervantesvirtual.com/

29. Project Gutenberg https://www.gutenberg.org/

30. Internet Archive https://archive.org/
31. Wikisource https://es.wikisource.org/
32. Amazon Kindle https://amzn.to/3yDKtjn
33. Apple Books https://www.apple.com/apple-books/
34. LibriVox https://librivox.org/
35. EBiblio https://www.cultura.gob.es/cultura/areas/bibliotecas/mc/eBiblio/inicio.html
36. Z-Library https://z-lib.id/
37. Elejandria https://www.elejandria.com/
38. Google Books https://books.google.es/
39. Textos.info https://www.textos.info/
40. Dominican Digital Library https://biblioteca.agn.gob.do/
41. Dominican Books in PDF https://issuu.com/librosdominicanosenpdf https://www.calameo.com/accounts/5815804
42. Dialnet https://dialnet.unirioja.es/
43. DOAB https://www.doabooks.org/
44. LISANews https://www.lisanews.org/

Tools and Softwares

45. **Hootsuite** Social Media Marketing and Management Tool (hootsuite.com) https://www.hootsuite.com/
46. **Buffer** Buffer: All-you-need social media toolkit for small businesses https://buffer.com/
47. **Brandwatch** Brandwatch Influence – Product Demo | Brandwatch https://www.brandwatch.com/

48. **Sprout Social** Sprout Social: Social Media Management Solutions https://sproutsocial.com/es/

49. **Talkwalker** Talkwalker - Leading Consumer Intelligence Platform https://www.talkwalker.com/es/

50. **Meltwater** Meltwater: Media, Social & Consumer Intelligence https://www.meltwater.com/en

51. **Crimson Hexagon** Brandwatch

52. **Palantir** https://www.palantir.com/

53. **Dataminr** Real-Time Event and Risk Detection - Dataminr https://www.dataminr.com/

54. **Media Sonar** Digital Risk Detection & Web Intelligence | Media Sonar https://mediasonar.com/

55. **Tableau** Business Intelligence and Analysis Software | Tableau https://www.tableau.com/es-es

56. **Domo** Domo Diagrams, Visualizations, and Dashboards https://www.domo.com/es/

57. **QlikView** QlikView – Powerful, interactive analytics and dashboards | Qlik https://www.qlik.com/es-es/

58. **DataCamp** Learn data science and artificial intelligence online | DataCamp https://www.datacamp.com/es

59. **CEPD** https://www.edpb.europa.eu/sme-data-protection-guide/home_en

60. **European Data Protection Board** (Binding decisions) https://www.edpb.europa.eu/our-work-tools/consistency-findings/binding-decisions_en

www.ingramcontent.com/pod-product-compliance
Lightning Source LLC
Chambersburg PA
CBHW071916210526
45479CB00002B/443